Heaven and Hell

- from different points of view

H H Osborn

Apologia

Copyright © H H Osborn 2009

All rights reserved

By the same author:

Fire in the Hills   Highland
Revival - God's Spotlight   Highland
Revival- A precious heritage   Apologia
Pioneers in the East African Revival   Apologia
The living legacy of the East African Revival   Apologia
The greatest story ever told   Apologia
God and the antelope in the bush   Apologia
The hidden key to the God-scenario   Apologia
An introduction to the Creation/Evolution confusion   Apologia

ISBN 978 1 901566 14 7

Unless otherwise stated, all Scripture quotations are from
The Holy Bible, English Standard Version. (Author's emphasis),
Harper Collins Publishers © 2001 by Crossway Bibles.
All rights reserved.

Apologia Publications
P.O. Box 3005
Eastbourne
East Sussex
BN21 9BS
UK

Printed and bound in Great Britain by
CPI Antony Rowe, Chippenham and Eastbourne

Contents

Introduction	An uncomfortable combination of ideas.....	5
1	A disturbing discovery	7
2	A discomforting realisation	15
3	A revolutionary conclusion	17
4	The defining destinies	21
5	The distinguishing natures	25
6	The determining choice	31
7	The great divide	37
8	The Harvest	47
9	Enjoyment and torment	59
10	The symbolism of heaven and hell	65
11	The two points of view	73
12	Conclusion	81
Epilogue	....	91
Appendix A	The two natures in three environments	109
Appendix B	Born *outside* the Kingdom of God	110
Appendix C	To be 'born again' into God's Kingdom	112

(Jesus) "But I say to you that everyone who is angry with his brother will be liable to judgement; ... and whoever says 'You fool!" will be liable to the hell of fire." [1]

(Jesus) "If your hand causes you to sin, cut it off. It is better for you to enter life crippled than with two hands to go to hell, to the unquenchable fire. ... And if your eye causes you to sin, tear it out. It is better for you to enter the kingdom of God with one eye than with two eyes to be thrown into hell where their worm does not die and the fire is not quenched." [2]

(Jesus) "Woe to you , Scribes and Pharisees, hypocrites ... You serpents, you brood of vipers, how are you to escape being sentenced to hell ..." [3]

(Jesus) "I tell you, my friends, do not fear those who kill the body, and after that have nothing more that they can do, But I will warn you whom to fear; fear him who, after he has killed, has authority to cast into hell. Yes. I tell you, fear him." [4]

(John, in Revelation) "Then I saw a great white throne and him who was seated on it. ... And I saw the dead, great and small, standing before the throne, and books were opened. Then another book was opened, which is the book of life. And the dead were judged by what was written in the books, according to what they had done. ... This is the second death, the lake of fire. And if anyone's name was not found written in the book of life, he was thrown into the lake of fire." [5]

[1] Matthew 5:22   [2] Mark 9:43-48   [3] Matthew 23:29-33
[4] Luke 12:4-5   [5] Revelation 20:11-15

Introduction

An uncomfortable combination of ideas

Heaven is a popular subject for Christians ... Hell is not!

That *heaven* is a popular theme is understandable. It is the promised destination of every Christian and it is described in the Bible in the most glowing terms. The theme of *hell* is rarely mentioned. There are two principle reasons for this:

(a) The Bible depicts hell (gehenna) as a state of unimaginable and everlasting pain and torment for 'unrepentant sinners', to be viewed with utmost fear and horror.

(b) It is difficult for Christians to imagine God, who is supremely love, able to enjoy heaven with the 'saints'— *the 'forgiven sinners'*— knowing that, at the same time, there are millions of people — *the unforgiven sinners* — enduring the unending torment of hell?

'Love' and 'hell' make an uncomfortable combination of ideas!

Preaching on the subject takes several different forms:

- some reject the idea of hell totally and believe that a God of love could only have one destination for everyone that He has brought into existence — *heaven*. Hence there is no need to be concerned about biblical references to hell.

- some portray the biblical descriptions of hell in vivid, literal and physical terms — fire, brimstone, unquenchable thirst, undying worms, everlasting torment. This terrible destiny is depicted in this way to urge repentance of sin and trust in Jesus Christ to escape from it.

- some describe the glories of heaven with little or no mention of any possible alternative. The significance of *hell* is ignored.

- some, while denying the literal physical interpretations of the biblical terms, urge an acceptance of their assumed spiritual symbolic significance on the grounds that, if they were not meant to be taken seriously, they would not be given such prominence in the Bible.

I, like many other Christians, have not been able to resolve the uncomfortable combination of ideas — *a God of love and a hell of everlasting torment.*

I have studied the proposals of the so-called 'conditional immortality' interpretation of Basil Atkinson of my student days, and of those who followed him, with no conviction of the validity of their arguments. I have read the very commendable "Whatever happened to hell?" by John Blanchard. I have listened to sermons on the subject. I have been happy to put on one side the, to me, uncomfortable combination of ideas about God's love and *hell* in the assurance expressed by Abraham: *"shall not the Judge of all the earth do what is just?"* [1]

That is ... *until now*!

---

[1] Genesis 18:25

Chapter 1

A disturbing discovery

A Christian background, such as I have enjoyed, carries with it the danger of unquestioned presuppositions which are often not recognized as such until exposed. That was my situation until I began to see a pattern of behaviour which I had not until then perceived.

The source of this discovery has been the many reports I have read in recent years of those who have perpetrated the most brutal atrocities on their fellow men and women; of leaders in positions of power who have mercilessly eliminated those who challenged their authority and inflicted terrible injustices on their victims; of countless soldiers who have mercilessly raped helpless women and young girls; of fathers and mothers who have cruelly abused their own and other children; of husbands who have brutally ill-treated their wives; of strong young men and women who have kicked and beaten those unable to defend themselves; of very rich people who live near to men, women and children in dire poverty; of business men who have defrauded their fellow human beings of vast sums of money, and millions of people who appear to live their lives without reference to God their Creator.

1 A disturbing discovery

There is nothing new in this behaviour. People have reportedly acted like that since the dawn of recorded history. The disturbing discovery for me was the startling revelation that those acting in these ways *enjoy* what they are doing! They *take pleasure* in their evil actions! They *delight* in the heinous mental and physical pain they cause! They *approve* of the oppression of the helpless! They *relish* the misery of those whom they are causing to suffer! They *rejoice* in their riches and power, unconcerned with the plight of the poor and helpless around them, they *approve* of, and even *promote* the denial of the existence of their Creator.

An incident in the story of President Saddam Hussein, recorded by the Iraqui General Georges Sada made a deep impression on me. An Iraqui medical doctor, Dr Raji, was reported as having criticized the President. He was called to Hussein's palace where:

> "... he was taken to a large room in the basement where the president's elite guards had their headquarters. ... Off to one side, Saddam was just sitting in a chair with his legs crossed. He took out a big Havana cigar and lit it, and he said to the soldiers, "Okay, do it." At that, one of the soldiers reached out and knocked Dr Raji to the ground. The others immediately moved in and started stomping him with their hob-nail boots, pounding, jumping, kicking, and crushing him to death right there on that floor. And while this was going on. Saddam just sat there, smoking his cigar. When the soldiers finished the grisly business, a guard opened the door of a kennel and unleashed a pack of dogs that had been starved for days. Those dogs consumed that poor man's body completely and licked up his blood from the floor." [1]

[1] Georges Sada *Saddam's Secrets* p.93

1 A disturbing discovery

The scene of Saddam Hussein sitting smoking a cigar while watching that act of utmost horror reminds me of a popular advertisement of the past: "Happiness is a cigar called Hamlet". I cannot avoid the conclusion that Saddam Hussein experienced *happiness* as he watched that abominable act.

Many, if not all, of the thousands of men and women who supported Hitler, Stalin, Pol Pot and others in their appalling atrocities appear to have been quite *happy* to do so. Sadistic behaviour — deriving pleasure as a result of inflicting pain, or watching pain inflicted — has a long history.

During the period of the Roman empire, it is recorded that thousands of men and women were killed in gladiatorial combats or by animals for the entertainment of the spectators. It is a fact of history that generations of people *enjoyed* the spectacle of men killing each other and of animals tearing apart their fellow human beings. Countless men and women have taken, and still take *pleasure* in watching similar spectacles of staged fighting between cockerels, dogs and other animals and birds.

I read recently of a medieval picture of a prisoner being brutally tortured while strapped to a chair. According to the commentator "The prisoner's eyes bulge with terror as he feels himself drowning" while the watching inquisitors betray not the slightest feelings of sympathy with the prisoner. They were clearly enjoying their experience.

Under the names of eugenics and medical research, the 20th century witnessed many thousands of men, women and children, who were considered as 'less than human', suffer the most cruel experiments at the hands of doctors who appeared not only to approve of what they were doing but actually taking pleasure in it.

As this horrific picture of human sadism has unfolded before me it has dawned on me with tremendous force that the millions of people who have in the past, and are today, inflicting grievous pain and perpetrating heinous atrocities do so with great *enjoyment, delight* and *pleasure*. Others, while not actively engaged in such despicable activities, approve the spectacle of them.

Some psychology researchers have, in the last century, investigated the possibility that the behaviour described could be traced to some inherited physical condition, a form of psychosis which reflects an inability or unwillingness to recognize and acknowledge reality and hence, to relate with others in real terms. This implies that such perpetrators of evil are not fully responsible for their actions. I find that diagnosis insufficient to explain the immensity of the evil. There is more to this behaviour than mental dysfunction.

My first reaction to these atrocities has been that of horror that ordinary men and women can act in what seem to me to be such depraved ways. I knew that leaders such as Stalin and Hitler had ordered heinous crimes but I had assumed that those who obeyed those commands had been acting against their better natures and that they had been acting under orders from their superiors.

My second reaction was to go to the Bible to see what light God has given on this issue.

I was not disappointed.

There are many references there to people *taking pleasure in ..., delighting in ..., rejoicing in ..., enjoying ..., being content to ...* and *approving* activities. The same words — *pleasure, delight, rejoicing, enjoyment, approval* and *contentment* — are used but those who experience them and the objects of their pleasure and enjoyment are very different.

1 A disturbing discovery

References to the enjoyment, delight and rejoicing of God's people in obeying Him and doing good are to be found throughout the Bible.

There are fewer references to the enjoyment of those whose behaviour is evil but they are sufficient to confirm that such is recognized.

* Speaking through the prophet Isaiah, God referred to the Jewish people of his day who twisted His laws: *"These have chosen their own ways, and their soul delights in their abominations."* [1]

And through Ezekiel: *"But as for those whose heart goes after their detestable things and their abominations, I will bring their deeds upon their own heads, declares the Lord GOD."* [2]

* The Psalms and Proverbs include references to those who enjoy their depraved actions

"You love evil more than good and lying more than speaking what is right." [3]

"How long will you love vain words and seek after lies." [4]

"They take pleasure in falsehood. They bless with their mouths but inwardly they curse" [5]

"Scatter the peoples who delight in war." [6]

"How long will scoffers delight in their scoffing and *fools hate knowledge."* [7]

* *"... men of perverted speech ... who rejoice in doing evil and delight in the perverseness of evil."* [8]

* *"Doing wrong is like a joke to a fool."* [9]

* Herod *"killed James the brother of John with the sword and when he saw that it pleased the Jews, he proceeded to arrest Peter also."* [10]

---

[1] Isaiah 66:3 [2] Ezekiel 11:21 [3] Psalm 52:2-4 [4] Psalm 4:2 [5] Psalm 62:4 [6] Psalm 68:30 [7] Proverbs 1:22 [8] Proverbs 2:14 [9] Proverbs 10:23 [10] Acts 12:2-3

1 A disturbing discovery

Herod was delighted to arrest Peter because his murder of James had given pleasure to the people. He enjoyed the praise and adulation of those who delighted in the execution of James.

* The Apostle Paul concludes a list of men and women who misused their sexuality and were:

"filled — permeated and saturated — with every kind of unrighteousness, iniquity, grasping and covetous greed ... though they are fully aware of God's righteous decree that those who do such things deserve to die, they not only do them themselves but approve and applaud others who practice them." [1]

To approve and applaud those who indulge in evil deeds is a clear indication of the pleasure such evil doers would enjoy in taking part in the same activities.

* Paul had, in fact, before his conversion, experienced what he was later to condemn. In his defence, after his arrest in Jerusalem, he said:

"And when the blood of Stephen your witness was being shed, I myself was standing by and approving and watching over the garments of those who killed him." [2]

* The Apostle Peter referred to people *"who indulge in the lust of defiling passion and despise authority ...But these, like irrational animals ... count it pleasure to revel in the daytime ... revelling in their deceptions."* [3]

* Paul wrote: *"Love ... does not rejoice at wrong doing..."* [4] well aware that there were those who do rejoice in wrong doing.

* And to Timothy: *"For people will be lovers of self, lovers of money ... lovers of pleasure rather than lovers of God."* [5]

[1] Romans 1:29-32 (Amplified)   [2] Acts 22:20   [3] 1 Peter 2:10-13
[4] 1 Corinthians 13:6   [5] 2 Timothy 3:2-4

1 A disturbing discovery

* The writer to the Hebrews wrote: *"Moses ... choosing rather to be mistreated with the people of God than to enjoy the fleeting pleasures of sin."* [1]

Evidence from secular sources provides ample evidence of the nature of the 'pleasures of sin' rejected by Moses.

* The final and most authoritative quotation is from the lips of Jesus:

"God did not send his Son into the world to condemn the world, ... this is the judgement: the light has come into the world, and people loved the darkness rather than light, because their deeds were evil." [2]

There are many references in the Bible to the *pleasure, delight, rejoicing, enjoyment* and *contentment,* that people experience in activities which are evil from God's point of view and not only taking part in them but giving their *approval* and *applause* to those who act in those ways.

I have read these passages many times. I have assumed that those engaged in such activities knowingly acted *against* their better natures. They knew that what they were doing was wrong because it was against the social order of life, but something in their natures made them overcome their logical reasoning and get enjoyment from what they really did not want to do.

It was at this point that I made the disturbing discovery that people who behave in such depraved and futile ways act not *against,* but *in accordance* with their natures. They are, in fact, behaving *naturally,* in the sense that what they do is in response to an inner urge for unrestricted freedom of action to gratify their natural desires.

That, in behaving in such depraved and futile ways, people act not *against* their nature, but *in accordance* with it, came as a disturbing discovery.

[1] Hebrews 11:25 [2] John 3:19

A recognition of the enjoyment of many people in committing evil deeds prompted a question which led to a further disturbing discovery. Was the pleasure many people gained in committing evil deeds an end in itself or were there other objectives?

It became very clear to me that while some evil acts were sadistic in that they brought immediate enjoyment in the experience of them, there were often further powerful sources of pleasure in achieving ends which could be either evil or futile. The example given of Saddam Hussein's brutal murder of Dr Raji was utterly sadistic. There was, however, a further motive, that of maintaining his political power. In spiritual terms, this aim was futile.

The fact became clear to me that many, if not most people enjoy activities which are, in spiritual terms, futile. Any gain from them is solely temporary. Many people expend much time and effort in gaining wealth beyond their needs, train their bodies to the limit in order to gain celebrity recognition, give great sums of money in order to gain social status, pray to idols made of wood, stone or metal with the imagined promise of an answer to their pleasing.

The application of the words of Jesus "where your treasure is your heart will be also," reveals that a very great deal of the 'treasure' where people's hearts are, is, in spiritual terms, imagined and futile. To use modern terminology, many people appear to live in a spiritual virtual reality.

The disturbing discovery for me was that, in *enjoying* evil actions, in *achieving* evil aims, in *applauding* the evil behaviour of others, and in pursuing spiritually *futile* activities, people act not *against*, but *according to* their natures.

Chapter 2

A discomforting realisation

There was only one conclusion that was open to me from the disturbing discovery I had made, that people act in evil ways not *against*, but *in accordance* with their natures. Those who delight in good, and those who delight in evil activities *could not be the same persons*. The two different perceptions of enjoyment must be those of two *different groups of people*.

The discomforting realisation for me was that the pleasure, delight and enjoyment that people experience is not a matter of the different attitudes of the *same* person. It was not that the Romans who attended the 'games' sometimes enjoyed seeing their fellow human being torn to pieces by animals and, at other times, were revolted by the spectacle. Those who enjoyed the spectacles and those who were revolted by them were *different people*.

The people who *take pleasure* in cruel actions are not the same as those who consider them loathsome. Some people *delight* causing heinous mental and physical pain while others abhor the very idea. Some people *approve* of the oppression of the powerless for their gain which others strongly disapprove. Some *rejoice* in their riches and power, unconcerned with the plight of the poor and helpless while others deplore that situation. Some people can be entertained by the spectacle of pain being inflicted on people or animals while others feel revulsion.

The inescapable conclusion is that such diametrically opposed points of view cannot be held by the same people. All men and women are in many aspects alike. Both have similar physical bodies with similar needs to maintain life and reproduce the species. Both are able to observe, think and react to events. Science cannot distinguish between them. There is only one part of a human being which can be the source of this distinguishing feature ... the *spirit*.

The conclusion is inescapable: people hold the different views of the same behaviour, not because of any physical variations, but because there are fundamental differences in their spiritual characters which are not discernible by any physical means. We refer to the spiritual characters of people as their 'spiritual natures'.

The way people judge behaviour depends on their point of view, and that, in turn, depends on their nature. This is part, at least, of what Jesus meant when He said:

"The eye is the lamp of the body. So, if your eye is healthy, your whole body will be full of light, but if your eye is bad, your whole body will be full of darkness. If then the light in you is darkness, how great is the darkness!" [1]

The 'eyes' — the 'spiritual natures' of some people are healthy and their whole outlook is 'full of light' while the 'eyes' — the 'spiritual natures' of others are unhealthy and their whole outlook on life is 'full of darkness'.

The discomforting realisation for me was that people are fundamentally different in their spiritual natures. Their differing behaviour and outlook are the natural expressions of their different 'spiritual natures'.

[1] Matthew 6:22-23

Chapter 3

A revolutionary conclusion

My discomforting realisation, that the different forms of behaviour and outlook of people are not variations in their thinking but are expressions of their different spiritual natures, was accompanied by a revolutionary conclusion: that the Bible presents things from one point of view:
— *God's point of view*.
I was driven to conclude that there was possibly another point of view:
— *the 'anti-God' point of view*.
Throughout the Bible, the views of moral issues — right and wrong, good and evil — are those which God has caused to be written for our benefit in that Book. To look at things from His point of view is to think as He thinks. Judgements on people's behaviour are those of our Creator-God. Both *heaven* and *hell* are described in the Bible from the point of view of a holy God. It is logical to presume, therefore, that His views will be held by those who are members of His family and share His nature.

The examples given above of those who *take pleasure in ...*, *delight in ...*, *rejoice in ...*, *enjoy* and *approve of* evil activities illustrate one point of view. When seen from the anti-God point of view, the activities do not change, but *the perception of them does*.

It is not difficult to imagine what might have been said by biblical characters whose natures were very different from that of God and whose points of view were, therefore, the opposite of His.

* I can imagine Satan saying about Job: "I hate seeing him so righteous, and successful. I would be very happy if he lost all his family and his possessions and I would be delighted to see him grovelling in the dust, scratching his sores and cursing God."

* It is not difficult to imagine Pharoah saying: "Of course I ordered the harsh treatment of those Israelites. Not only did I approve of what my people did to them, for their slavery was profitable for the Egyptian economy, but it gave me great pleasure to see them forced to make bricks! I hated to see them go."

* In the book of Esther, Haman, having been promoted to a very high official position by King Ahasuerus gained permission from him to kill all the Jews. It is reported that he *"went out that day joyful and glad of heart."* [1] He was, metaphorically speaking, rubbing his hands with glee at the prospect of mass murder.

* It is not difficult to imagine that it was with great enthusiasm and approval that the Jews shouted "Crucify Him!" when Jesus stood before Pilate. Particularly would this apply to the religious leaders who saw Jesus as a threat to their teaching and authority. It probably gave them great satisfaction to see Him suffering for His challenge.

* I can imagine the Jewish "people, elders and the scribes" at Jerusalem reporting the murder of Stephen: "We were fed up with all that 'holier than thou' stuff from him. It was a pleasure to stone him to death."

[1] Esther 5:9

3 A revolutionary conclusion

* It is not difficult to picture the philosophy debators of the Areopagus who spent *"their time in nothing except telling or hearing something new"* [1] mocking Paul. "He is a fool," I can imagine them saying, "no one can know anything for certain". In so saying they would reveal how they revelled in the futility of their thinking.

It is a fact of history, as of life today, that there are many people who, in the past and in the present, enjoy giving pleasure to others, who delight in relieving the oppressed and approve of helping the helpless, who use their time for praiseworthy ends, who delight in using their mental abilities to investigate the universe and translate its capabilities for the benefit of their fellows.

At the same time there are many who enjoy seeing others in pain, who take delight in torturing innocent victims, who take pleasure in benefitting from the oppression or poverty of others, who spend a great deal of time in activities which, while not being evil, serve only themselves and are, therefore, spiritually futile.

The revolutionary conclusion for me was that (a) those who enjoy activities which are good and beneficial to others are *not the same people* who enjoy activities which are evil and cause pain to others, and (b) the activities enjoyed by people are the expression of their *different natures*.

Mention must be made of situations which I found difficult at first to fit into these conclusions. I understand that Stalin was very happy to enjoy the fun of being with his family at the same time as he was ordering the elimination of men he deemed his enemies. During World War 2, guards in the German extermination camps enjoyed happy family and social gatherings among themselves at the same time as perpetrating the horrendous crimes of the holocaust.

[1] Acts 17:21

3 A revolutionary conclusion

How does this fit in with my conclusion that the people who enjoy committing heinous crimes are not the same as those who delight in giving pleasure to others?

The answer leaves no room for doubt. Stalin did not enjoy the pleasure of the company of those he hated. The guards at the extermination camps did not take delight in the company of those they were eliminating. The enjoyment and pleasure experienced in these situations was totally self-centred.

The word 'enjoyment' may be applied to both those who take pleasure in giving happiness to others and to those who seek solely the gratification of their own self-centred interests, but the form of the enjoyment and the natures of those who experience it are very different

In its utterly truthful reporting of human activities and the natures they express, the Bible confirms the pleasure that some enjoy in doing good and others enjoy in doing evil.

There is a popular saying;

"One man's *meat* is another man's *poison*."

Could it be that

"One man's *torment* is another man's *pleasure*" ?
"One man's *torture* is another man's *delight*" ?
"One man's *agony* is another man's *entertainment*?

Or, to push this further:

"One man's *hell* is another man's *heaven*" ?

Is this possible?

Chapter 4

The defining destinies

The Bible has a great deal to say about two groups of people whose natures are very different. A variety of terms are used to describe them — 'righteous' and 'unrighteous', 'godly', and 'ungodly'. It is assumed that readers will be aware of their meanings. Here, for the sake of simplicity, the terms *unforgiven sinners* and *forgiven sinners* will be used as being understandable by most readers.

In the Bible, the most frequent allusions to these two groups of people associate them with their final destinies. To put it in blunt terms, one group, the 'forgiven sinners', will, after death, go to *heaven,* and the others, the 'unforgiven sinners' will go to *hell.*

For purposes of clarity, the terms 'heaven' and 'heavens' have two distinct meanings. The appropriate sense is usually clear from the context. In the Hebrew understanding, the 'first heaven' is the atmosphere above the earth. The second heaven is space beyond the atmosphere to the stars. These together constitute the heavens. King David proclaimed:

"The heavens declare the glory of God, and the sky above proclaims his handiwork." [1]

[1] Psalm 19:1

4 The defining destinies

Depending on the context, 'heaven', singular, refers to the 'eternal dwelling place of God'. This was the Hebrew 'third heaven'. Paul referred to this when he recorded that he was *"caught up to the third heaven—whether in the body or out of the body I do not know, God knows."* [1]

The common usage is maintained in which 'heaven' usually refers to the spiritual realm where God is, and the 'heavens' refer to the space, from the atmosphere around the earth to the farthest galaxy of stars.

The fact of a coming 'great divide' is inescapable:

* In an early prophecy, Enoch foretold a coming judgement to separate the 'godly' from the 'ungodly' people:

"Behold, the Lord comes with ten thousands of his holy ones, to execute judgment on all and to convict all the ungodly of all their deeds of ungodliness that they have committed in such an ungodly way, and of all the harsh things that ungodly sinners have spoken against him." [2]

* God revealed to the prophet Daniel centuries before the birth of Jesus Christ:

"And many of those who sleep in the dust of the earth shall awake, some to everlasting life, and some to shame and everlasting contempt." [3]

* Jesus spoke in parables of this division of people and their respective destinies:

"Again, the kingdom of heaven is like a net that was thrown into the sea and gathered fish of every kind. When it was full, men drew it ashore and sat down and sorted the good into containers but threw away the bad. So it will be at the close of the age. The angels will come out and separate the evil from the righteous and throw them into the fiery furnace. In that place there will be weeping and gnashing of teeth." [4]

[1] 2 Corinthians 12:2 [2] Jude 14-15 [3] Daniel 12:2 [4] Matthew 13:47-50

* In another parable, Jesus referred to one group as 'wheat' or 'good seed' and to the other as 'weeds' that had been planted by an enemy :

"Let both grow together until the harvest, and at harvest time I will tell the reapers, Gather the weeds first and bind them in bundles to be burned, but gather the wheat into my barn. ... The field is the world, and the good seed is the sons of the kingdom. The weeds are the sons of the evil one, and the enemy who sowed them is the devil. The harvest is the close of the age, and the reapers are angels. Just as the weeds are gathered and burned with fire, so will it be at the close of the age. The Son of Man will send his angels, and they will gather out of his kingdom all causes of sin and all law-breakers, and throw them into the fiery furnace. In that place there will be weeping and gnashing of teeth. Then the righteous will shine like the sun in the kingdom of their Father. He who has ears, let him hear." [1]

* Jesus left no doubt as to the destiny of the people of 'all the nations of the world'. When He comes to earth again he will divide them into two groups —the 'sheep' and the 'goats', the 'blessed' and the 'cursed'.

"When the Son of Man comes in his glory, and all the angels with him, then he will sit on his glorious throne. Before him will be gathered all the nations, and he will separate people one from another as a shepherd separates the sheep from the goats. And he will place the sheep on his right, but the goats on the left. Then the King will say to those on his right, 'Come you who are blessed by my Father, into the kingdom prepared for you from the foundation of the world' ... Then he will say to those on his left, 'Depart from me, you cursed, into the eternal fire prepared for the devil and his angels.'" [2]

[1] Matthew 13:30,38-43 [2] Matthew 25:31-41

However difficult it may appear for the biblical teaching on *heaven* and *hell* to be included in preaching the Gospel, there is no doubt that without it the Gospel is incomplete. It is a matter of spiritual life and death for ever. The choice of destiny is made in this life and it is at the heart of the Gospel.

The 'great divide' between the two groups of people is characterised by differences in (a) their spiritual natures. (b) their behaviour in this life and (c) their final destinations after physical life.

We can now go a stage further and recognize that the two groups will also *see things from different points of view* and this will include their views of *heaven* and *hell*. It follows that an understanding of the two different spiritual natures is necessary for an understanding of their different points of view.

Chapter 5

The destinguishing natures

The great upheaval in my thinking has been the result of a much greater understanding of the extent of the differences in the natures of Christians — the *forgiven sinners,* and of non-Christians — the *unforgiven sinners*, and the effects of those differences in this and the life after physical death.

There are a number of terms which are used to describe the natures of the non-Christian and the Christian. It is beyond the scope of this small book to expound the depth of meaning of these terms in the Bible. They are listed here as a suggestion for further study:

Non-Christian	**Christian**
Unsaved	Saved
'Of the flesh', carnal	'Of the spirit', spiritual
The 'natural man'	The 'spiritual man'
The 'old self'	The 'new self'
The Fallen nature	The Redeemed nature
Unregenerate	Regenerate
The 'old man'	The 'new man'
'Dead in sin'	'Alive in the Spirit'
Depraved	Renewed
Lovers of darkness	Lovers of light
Saint	Unholy
Slave	Son
Lost	Found

Something very radical and fundamental happens to the man or woman who is 'born again' or 'born anew' into the kingdom or family of God. The words: 'life' and 'death' refer to both physical and spiritual experiences. A *'man'* — male or female, is *physically dead or alive* depending on whether or not there is air passing through his or her body to maintain life. A *'man'* — male or female, is *spiritually dead* or *alive* depending on whether or not the Spirit of God is passing through his or her spirit to maintain spiritual life.

In the incident already quoted, Jesus said to Nicodemus:

"The wind blows where it wishes, and you hear its sound, but you do not know where it comes from or where it goes. So it is with everyone who is born of the Spirit." [1]

Jesus here describes a person who is 'born of the Spirit' as being like a tree through the branches of which blows the wind. Although invisible, the wind is essential to maintain the life of the tree. So it is with 'born again' Christians. The Spirit of God, equally invisible to the human eye, figuratively 'blows' through their spirits to give spiritual life. The difference between one who is, and one who is not 'born again' into the kingdom of God, is physically invisible but is as real as physical life is different from physical death.

The Apostle Paul spelled out the difference: *"And you were dead in the trespasses and sins in which you once walked, following the course of this world, following the prince of the power of the air, the spirit that is now at work in the sons of disobedience— among whom we all once lived in the passions of our flesh, carrying out the desires of the body and the mind, and were by nature children of wrath, like the rest of mankind. But God, being rich in mercy, because of the great love with which he loved us, even when*

[1] John 3:8

we were dead in our trespasses, made us alive together with Christ— by grace you have been saved— and raised us up with him and seated us with him in the heavenly places in Christ Jesus, so that in the coming ages he might show the immeasurable riches of his grace in kindness toward us in Christ Jesus. For by grace you have been saved through faith. And this is not your own doing; it is the gift of God, not a result of works, so that no one may boast. For we are his workmanship, created in Christ Jesus for good works, which God prepared beforehand, that we should walk in them." [1]

Using the language of Paul, the nature of the person who is 'spiritually dead' is called *'the old self'*. The living tree with the air blowing through its branches is like a person who is 'alive spiritually' with the Spirit of God figuratively 'blowing' through and maintaining his or her life. That person's nature is *'the new self'*.

"Do not lie to one another, seeing that you have put off the old self with its practices and have put on the new self, which is being renewed in knowledge after the image of its creator." [2]

A dead tree needs no air. A living one does!

According to the Apostle Paul, the 'fallen' nature is self-centred and is incapable of thinking or doing anything that is, in God's scale of values, good. He put it like this:

"For I know that nothing good dwells in me, that is, in my flesh (fallen nature). *For I have the desire to do what is right, but not the ability to carry it out."* [3]

During this life, God acts on our spirits giving us a conscience — consciousness of what is right and what is wrong, what is real and what is futile — and a desire to act in ways which are good and have lasting value.

[1] Ephesians 2:1-10 [2] Colossians 3:9-10 [3] Romans 7:18

5 The distinguisging natures

Paul continued:

"For I delight in the law of God in my inner being, but I see in my members, another law, waging war against the law of my mind and making me captive to the law of sin that dwells in my members." [1]

The person who is not 'in Christ', to use Paul's expression, has a character or disposition that is self-centred and, although understanding who God is, ignores Him in self-interest. To accept a Creator-God to whom one is responsible and the interests of others before one's own, is not natural for the 'fallen nature'. Being 'dead in sin' can be stated as being separated from the life of God and all that is God's character — holiness, light (openness) and love (the commitment always to put others before oneself).

That is what the Apostle Paul meant when he wrote about Jews and Gentiles:

"For there is no distinction; for all have sinned and fall short of the glory of God." [2]

God's glory is His perfect holiness, perfect light (openness with others) and perfect love (commitment to others).

In theological circles, the word 'depraved' is used to describe the way the perfect nature with which God created the first man and woman — Adam and Eve — was corrupted when they disobeyed Him.

Before we become 'born again' Christians, we are subject, *internally*, to our 'fallen' depraved, corrupted natures and *externally* to the influence on us of both God and the adversary Satan.

When we become truly Christian, we still have our 'fallen' natures, but we become so united with God that both the expression 'in Him' and 'He in us' apply. He influences Christians *internally*.

[1] Romans 7:22-23 [2] Romans 3:23

5 The distinguisging natures

To change the metaphor to one Jesus uses elsewhere, Christians become branches of the tree which is Jesus. In the first picture, it is the wind which gives life to the tree, in the second it is the sap which flows through the trunk to the branches. These are pictures drawn from the natural world to describe the same spiritual truths. All these descriptions of the 'unsaved' and 'unsaved' people indicate a radical difference in their natures.

A clear contrast between the natures of 'forgiven sinners' and 'unforgiven sinners' is given in Paul's letter to the Galatians. In this he contrasts the relationship of a slave to his master compared to that of a son to his father:

"I mean that the heir, as long as he is a child, is no different from a slave, though he is the owner of everything, but he is under guardians and managers until the date set by his father. In the same way we also, when we were children, were enslaved to the elementary principles of the world. But when the fullness of time had come, God sent forth his Son, born of woman, born under the law, to redeem those who were under the law, so that we might receive adoption as sons. And because you are sons, God has sent the Spirit of his Son into our hearts, crying, "Abba! Father!" So you are no longer a slave, but a son, and if a son, then an heir through God." [1]

In the context of this world, everyone is born as a *"slave ... to the elementary principles of the world"*. When a person is 'born again' or adopted into the family of God, He sends *"the Spirit of his Son into our hearts"* and he or she is *"no longer a slave, but a son, and if a son, then an heir through God."*

The transformation from 'slave' to 'son' is the most fundamental change that anyone can experience.

[1] Galatians 4:1-7

5 The distinguisging natures

The difference in nature between those who have, and those who have not, been 'born again' into the kingdom of God expresses itself in two ways. 'Born again' Christians have God's law 'written on their hearts', that is, their motivation is from God, *and* they live spiritually in a real world with real spiritual consequences. Those who are not 'born again' Christians know of God's law, at least through their consciences, but it is not 'written in their hearts' *and* they live in an unreal world with futile consequences.

There is a great deal written in the Bible about the evil in people's natural natures. The futile effects of living in a spiritually unreal world are there but are not so evident in ordinary life — worshipping imagined gods, working for wealth for wealth's sake, striving for power over fellow human beings, seeking celebrity status.

It is only when there is an understanding of the differences in the natures of 'unforgiven sinners' — the 'slaves', and 'forgiven sinners' — the 'sons', that it is possible to grasp the contrast between the experience of *heaven* and that of *hell,* and of the way they are viewed differently. The destinies of *heaven* and *hell* are not simply those of the same natured people existing in two very different environments.

The environment of *heaven* will be very different from that of *hell*. Equally different will be the natures of the *forgiven sinners* who occupy *heaven* from those of the *unforgiven sinners* who occupy *hell*.

Chapter 6

The determining choice

Every one is born a man or a woman — a *spirit* being with a *physical* body. The important fact which the Bible declares is that there is nothing wrong with a person's physical body. To make this absolutely clear, Jesus, the Son of God, was born into a human body and in it He lived a perfect, blameless life. However, when a baby is born, although capable of, in spirit, being *united* to God, he or she is *separated* from Him.

For more information on the biblical explanation of how it came about that people are born in the 'kingdom of Satan', and not in the 'kingdom of God' see Appendix B.

Everyone is born physically *alive* but spiritually *dead*, that is, spiritually separated from the life of God and with *hell* as their destiny. The good news of the Gospel is that it is God's intention that all who are 'born spiritually dead', that is spiritually 'separated from Him', should be 'born again' to be spiritually alive', that is 'united with Him' and, after physical death, spend eternity with Him in *heaven*.

For those who are familiar with computer language, *hell* is the 'default' destination of everyone. For the destiny to be *heaven* a person has to be 'customised' by Jesus. That 'customisation' is what Jesus achieved on the Cross.

6 The determining choice

As a baby is said to be *'born into the physical world'* so this transformation is referred to as being *'born again into the Kingdom of God.'* Jesus spelled this out in His talk with the Jewish leader Nicodemus. Here is the record for those who have never read it.

Jesus said to Nicodemus:

"Truly, truly, I say to you, unless one is born again he cannot see the kingdom of God." Nicodemus said to him, "How can a man be born when he is old? Can he enter a second time into his mother's womb and be born?" Jesus answered, "Truly, truly, I say to you, unless one is born of water and the Spirit, he cannot enter the kingdom of God. That which is born of the flesh is flesh, and that which is born of the Spirit is spirit. Do not marvel that I said to you, 'You must be born again.' The wind blows where it wishes, and you hear its sound, but you do not know where it comes from or where it goes. So it is with everyone who is born of the Spirit." [1]

Here Jesus explains that being 'born again' into the Kingdom of God is a spiritual experience — as real but also as invisible as the wind blowing in the trees. The transformation from being a non-Christian to a Christian is much greater that most people realize. The difference lies in the way that the change affects people's natures and behaviour now, the way they see things in this life and their future environments in *heaven* or *hell*.

(a) A person becomes a 'new creation'

The Apostle Paul wrote:

"For the love of Christ controls us, because we have concluded this: that one has died for all, therefore all have died; and he died for all, that those who live might no longer live for themselves but for him who for their sake died

[1] John 3:3-8

and was raised. From now on, therefore, we regard no one according to the flesh ... if anyone is in Christ, he is a new creation. The old has passed away; behold, the new has come." [1]

A person who is 'born again' spiritually is as much a 'new creation' as is physically the new born baby. As a 'new creation', he or she is much more than someone who has a change of mind, or acquires new information which affects the way he or she lives. As the physical elements which constitute a new born baby are there before air enters his or her body to make a living human being, so the spirit of a person ,who is born separated from God, is there before God's spirit enters him or her to make a 'new creation'.

(b) A person passes from *death* (separation from God) to *life* (union with God).

As previously mentioned, in the Bible, the words 'life' and 'death' have two meanings — the 'physical life and death' which everyone experiences and the 'spiritual life and death which mean 'union with' or 'separation from' the life of God.

Jesus said:

"Whoever hears my word and believes him who sent me has eternal life. He does not come into judgement but has passed from death to life." [2]

The change from being *spiritually* dead to being *spiritually alive* happens when a person is 'born again' into the Kingdom of God, It is as fundamental a change in the world of the spirit as is being born in the physical world.

(c) Christ 'in you' and 'you in Christ'

The death and resurrection of Jesus made possible a relationship with God that had not been possible before then. The tremendous truth, hidden until then, was that God was

[1] 2 Corinthians 5:14-18   [2] John 5:24

going to be in a far more intimate relationship with those who trusted in Him than was possible before then; He had been *with* them. He was thereafter going to be *in* them. The Apostle Paul referred to this. Referring to the 'church' — the body of all true Christians:

"... of which I became a minister according to the stewardship from God that was given to me for you, to make the word of God fully known, the mystery hidden for ages and generations but now revealed to his saints. To them God chose to make known how great among the Gentiles are the riches of the glory of this mystery, which is Christ in you, the hope of glory." [1]

Jesus made this specific point which would come into operation after His death and resurrection:

*"If you love me, you will keep my commandments. And I will ask the Father, and he will give you another Helper, to be with you forever, even the Spirit of truth, whom the world cannot receive, because it neither sees him nor knows him. You know him, for he dwells **with** you and will be **in** you."* [2]

Jesus prayed: *"I do not ask for these only, but also for those who will believe in me through their word, that they may all be one, just as you, Father, are in me, and I in you, that they also may be in us, so that the world may believe that you have sent me. The glory that you have given me I have given to them, that they may be one even as we are one, **I in them and you in me**, that they may become perfectly one, so that the world may know that you sent me and loved them even as you loved me."* [3]

Jesus spelled this out even more clearly:

"If anyone loves me, he will keep my word, and my Father will love him, and we will come to him and make our home with him." [4]

---

[1] Colossians 1:25-27   [2] John 14:15-17   [3] John 17:20-23   [4] John 14:23

(d) God writes His law on the hearts of those who are 'born again' into His Kingdom.

Centuries before the first coming of Christ, God made a promise through the prophet Jeremiah to His people, Israel, a promise which was later extended to all Christians who are 'grafted in' to Israel.

"This is the covenant that I will make with the house of Israel after those days, says the LORD: I will put my law within them, and I will write it on their hearts; and I will be their God and they will be my people." [1]

At conversion, when a man or woman is 'born again' into the 'kingdom of God' and they become 'in Christ' and 'Christ in them', God changes their natures and He writes into them a new motivation. The Ten Commandments which everyone is commanded to keep, become a way of life that the Christian wants above all else to follow. The *"I must keep the law ..."* becomes *"I want to keep the law."*

This radical change is illustrated by the story of a non-Christian who owned a fast car. He complained that he was not free to drive as fast as he wanted to because of all the speed limitations. He became a Christian. "I now know," he said, "that I was not free because what I wanted to do broke the law. Now, when I see a speed limit sign, I am free to take my foot off the accelerator and slow down to obey the law. I now want to do what I was then made to do."

At conversion, a person is radically changed, even if that is not visibly evident. The divide between those who are truly Christian and those who are not, begins in this life. Christians and non-Christians differ not only in name and in what they believe but also in what they *are*. Their natures are far more different than is commonly realized.. Christians have a 'fallen nature' from birth, but God enters their

[1] Jeremiah 31:33

lives to make them, as the Apostle Peter stated it, *"partakers of the divine nature"* [1] The event of God entering a person's life to be 'born again' into the 'kingdom of God' takes place in a moment. The process of transforming a 'fallen nature *without* God', referred to as 'perishing', into a 'fallen nature *with* God', referred to as 'sanctification' or being 'made holy' or 'perfect', goes on throughout life.

The Bible makes very clear, and the evidence of the way people behave in the world confirms that everyone belongs to one of two groups — the 'unrighteous', the 'unforgiven sinners', and the 'made righteous', the 'forgiven sinners', and their behaviour corresponds to their spiritual natures.

The *unrighteous* person has a nature which is *separated* from the life of God but is influenced by Him 'from outside' his or her spirit. The *made righteous* person has a 'fallen nature' but is *united* with God in spirit and is influenced by Him 'from the inside'.

The importance of the *determining choice* for a person is that it leads (a) to a transformation of his or her nature, (b) a change in behaviour, (c) a different outlook on life, and (d) a final destination of *heaven* or *hell*.

---

[1] 2 Peter 1:4

Chapter 7

The great divide

Physical death marks the end of a person's life on earth as it is now. The exception will be those Christians who are alive when, according to the Apostle Paul, Jesus comes for those who are His:

"For the Lord himself will descend from heaven with a cry of command, with the voice of an archangel, and with the sound of the trumpet of God. And the dead in Christ will rise first. Then we who are alive, who are left, will be caught up together with them in the clouds to meet the Lord in the air, and so we will always be with the Lord." [1]

The final determining event in the life of everyone will be what the Bible refers to as the Judgement of the Great White Throne. The Apostle John was given a vision of this event:

"Then I saw a great white throne and him who was seated on it. From his presence earth and sky fled away, and no place was found for them. And I saw the dead, great and small, standing before the throne, and books were opened.

---

[1] 1 Thessalonians 4:16-17

7 The great divide

Then another book was opened, which is the book of life. And the dead were judged by what was written in the books, according to what they had done. And the sea gave up the dead who were in it, Death and Hades gave up the dead who were in them, and they were judged, each one of them, according to what they had done. Then Death and Hades were thrown into the lake of fire. This is the second death, the lake of fire. And if anyone's name was not found written in the book of life, he was thrown into the lake of fire." [1]

It will be at this event that the separations referred to in Chapter 4 will be fulfilled — the 'godly' from the 'ungodly', the sheep from the goats, the wheat (good seed) from the weeds, the good fish from the bad, and those on the 'left' from those on the 'right'.

The distinguishing qualification of those on each side of the divide — *forgiven sinners* and the *unforgiven sinners* — will be whether or not their names are written in God's 'book of life'. Those on each side of the divide will then go to their respective destinies — *heaven* for the *forgiven sinners* and *hell* for the *unforgiven sinners*.

The two forms of the 'great divide'

The 'great divide', although one event, will take two forms. It will divide:

(a) *two environments* — *heaven* and *hell*. These are realms of the spirit with no stated physical locations.

(b) people of two *natures* — that of 'forgiven sinners' and that of 'unforgiven sinners'.

Fully to grasp the extent of the 'great divide' it is necessary to understand what the Bible reveals about both the *environments* of heaven and hell and of the *natures* of those who will occupy them.

[1] Revelation 20:11-15

The great divide between —
(a) *the environments of heaven and hell.*

Although the Bible does not define them in scientific terms, there are three environments clearly identified in the Bible.

(1) The spiritual environment of this present world:
  (a) God and Satan are present and influence people invisibly; [1]
  (b) people who are in the 'family of God' and those in the 'family of Satan' live in the same physical universe without physical distinction.
  (c) spiritual 'light' and 'darkness' (knowledge of the spirit world) coexist in people's minds.

Everyone in our present spiritual environment is influenced by God's presence in the world and by His control of all that happens, whether they are aware of it or not:

"For the grace of God has appeared, bringing salvation for all people," [2]

God is love (total commitment), light (openness), holy, compassionate — all the evidence that we see of these characteristics in our society have their source in Him.

"Every good gift and every perfect gift is from above, coming down from the Father of lights with whom there is no variation or shadow due to change." [3]

The Apostle Paul encouraged Christians to:

"Work out your salvation with fear and trembling, for it is God who works in you, both to will and to work for his good pleasure." [4]

This world is also under the influence of God's great adversary, Satan, whom He permits to operate under His 'permissive will' to demonstrate life in his family.

---
[1] See author's *The hidden key to the God scenario* Apologia
[2] Titus 2:11 [3] James 1:17 [4] Philippians 2:12

7 The great divide

The spiritual environment as people experience it in the world now allows them to fulfil their natural desires within the restrictions of the social order in which they live. People, left to themselves, are self-centred — greedy, envious, deceitful, unmerciful. This kind of behaviour is encouraged by Satan, the head of the family into which all are born.

There are many people today who behave in a decent, orderly way because, in our present environment, the cultural social limitations of imposed laws and the desire for self-preservation make it advantageous for them to do so. God planned for society to be organized that way. There is strong evidence that people act very differently when there is no law or order.

In the present spiritual environment everyone is influenced *externally* by both God and Satan, social circumstances and by the behaviour of others, and *internally,* by God in 'born again' Christians, and by Satan in those possessed by him.

(2) The spiritual environment of the future heaven:
   (a) God will be present *in* and *among* His people;
   (b) Everything will be 'in the light' as God's presence will illumine everywhere;
   (c) Neither Satan nor anything contrary to God's character will be there to influence people.

The best biblical description of heaven is the Apostle John's account in the book of Revelation:

"Then I saw a new heaven and a new earth, for the first heaven and the first earth had passed away, and the sea was no more. And I saw the holy city, new Jerusalem, coming down out of heaven from God, prepared as a bride adorned for her husband. And I heard a loud voice from the throne saying, "Behold, the dwelling place of God is with man. He

will dwell with them, and they will be his people, and God himself will be with them as their God. He will wipe away every tear from their eyes, and death shall be no more, neither shall there be mourning, nor crying, nor pain any more, for the former things have passed away. ... But nothing unclean will ever enter it, nor anyone who does what is detestable or false, but only those who are written in the Lamb's book of life." [1]

In heaven, for those who *are* 'children of God', He will be ever present and there will be no obstacles to a perfect eternal enjoyment *with Him* of all the God-given 'desires' and 'will' which have become theirs.

The Apostle John wrote:

"No man hath seen God at any time, the only begotten Son, which is in the bosom of the Father, he hath declared him." [2]

In *heaven* Christians will be with Jesus in the relationship, security and intimacy associated with being in the 'bosom of God the Father'.

(3) The spiritual environment of the future hell:
(a) Satan and his angels will be present.
(b) People will be free to fulfill all the spiritual desires of their natural selves;
(c) Total 'spiritual darkness' — separation from God.

The environment of those who are not 'children of God' — *hell* — is not so clearly defined in the Bible. There are, however, a number of important clues.

The Apostle John wrote:

"... and the devil who had deceived them (the nations) was thrown into the lake of fire and sulphur." [3] *"And if anyone's name was not found written in the book of life, he was thrown into the lake of fire."* [4]

[1] Revelation 21:1-4,21-27 [2] John 1:18 KJV [3] Revelation 20:10 [4] Revelation 20:21

7 The great divide

As God and His angels will be with His people in *heaven*, so Satan and his evil spirits will be with his people in *hell*.

The Apostle Paul, gives an important key:

"The righteous judgement of God ...when the Lord Jesus is revealed from heaven with his mighty angels in flaming fire, inflicting vengeance on those who do not know God and on those who do not obey the gospel of our Lord Jesus. They will suffer the punishment of eternal destruction, separated from the presence of the Lord and from the glory of his might, when he comes on that day to be glorified in his saints." [1]

The 'vengeance' of God refers to the punishment that those will suffer who have committed evil deeds and are unrepentant in this life. This will be proportional to the evil committed, and will end when completed. 'Eternal destruction' refers to the eternal separation from God which is the effect of their insistence on living independently of Him.

Those who, in this life are 'spiritually dead' and who are, therefore, already separated from Him, will, in *hell*, find that separation from His immediate presence complete, and also by the absence of all the good which His influence brought to them while physically alive. There will be no obstacles to a full eternal enjoyment of all that their fallen natures 'desire' and 'will' to do, *without Him.*

The term which is repeatedly used to describe the environment of hell is 'darkness'. Jesus referred to the Israelites as "sons of the kingdom" when He said:

"I tell you, many will come from east and west and recline at table with Abraham, Isaac, and Jacob in the kingdom of heaven, while the sons of the kingdom will be thrown into the outer darkness. In that place there will be weeping and gnashing of teeth." [2]

[1] 2 Thessalonians 1:9-10   [2] Matthew 8:11-12

7 The great divide

The Apostle Paul, addressing Christians, wrote:
"He (God) *has delivered us from the domain of darkness and transferred us to the kingdom of his beloved Son."* [1]

Physical darkness means the absence of physical light and therefore an inability to see what is there. 'Spiritual darkness' is an absence of 'spiritual truth', an inability to see what God has revealed — by conscience, by God's law spelled out by Moses and by the 'grace and truth' of Jesus.

Centuries of human history testify to the nature and consequences of this 'darkness': wars provoked by greed and the love of power, abuse of people to gratify the 'lusts of the flesh', fighting resulting from the hatred of one group for another, poverty of the 'have nots' resulting from the selfish acquisition of wealth by the 'haves', the futility of worshipping objects with imagined powers to change people's situations, the futile striving for applause and fame.

Human nature reveals its true character in many situations in society today where there is a breakdown of law and order, where government legislation leaves loopholes for people to act unlawfully in their own interests, where family life provides opportunities for unseen abuse of husbands, wives and children, and where commercial organisation includes activities which result in an unfair distribution of wealth.

The outworking of natural human nature is evident in many less obvious situations: bullying in the school play ground, spiteful comments in the office, vindictive behaviour in the factory, ethnic discrimination in job selection, plagiarism in the academic sphere, the falsification of research findings by scientists, sexual harassment in business relationships, pernicious insinuations in social conversation. All these give an insight into the 'domain of darkness'.

[1] Colossians 1:13

The great divide between —
(b) the *'unforgiven sinners'* and the *'forgiven sinners*

After physical death, some changes will happen to everyone whether they are Christians or not, that is, whether or not their names are written in the 'book of life'.

The Apostle Paul spelled this out:

"Behold! I tell you a mystery. We shall not all sleep, but we shall all be changed, in a moment, in the twinkling of an eye, at the last trumpet. For the trumpet will sound, and the dead will be raised imperishable, and we shall be changed. For this perishable body must put on the imperishable, and this mortal body must put on immortality. When the perishable puts on the imperishable, and the mortal puts on immortality, then shall come to pass the saying that is written: 'Death is swallowed up in victory. O death, where is your victory? O death, where is your sting?" [1]

From this it is clear that everyone will have eternal spirit bodies. All will no longer have the fear of physical death, although spiritual death remains for 'unforgiven sinners'. All will have full knowledge of their situations without the limits of physical minds.

The Apostle Paul ended his well-known statement on the way of love with the words:

"For now we see in a mirror dimly, but then face to face. Now I know in part; then I shall know fully even as I have been fully known." [2]

The Greek words translated *'I shall fully know'* and *'I have been fully known'* are usually understood to mean that, after physical death, what we know now will be increased by much more information about God and His working in us during this life. The great amount of research that is being carried out in medical science into the chemical means

---

[1] 1 Corinthians 15:51-55 [2] 1 Corinthians 13:12

of improving the capacity of the brain to function, points to the human mind being limited, not only in the extent of the knowledge it can absorb, but also in its ability to handle that knowledge. That the human mind is capable of observing and reasoning in very complex ways is demonstrated by some of the great minds of history — Isaac Newton and Albert Einstein come to mind.

As mental activity takes place in the human brain, it is logical to assume that, in this life, the ability to think is subject to the limitations of the human brain. After death, when the physical mortal bodies of people are transformed into immortal spirit bodies, the spiritual mind will not be limited by the physical brain. It will be capable of much greater reasoning and understanding.

In Paul's statement quoted above, he does not limit to himself the greater knowledge and ability to understand because he is a 'child of God'. It follows therefore, that those who are not 'children of God', will also have a much greater ability to understand and retain a much greater range of knowledge than is possible for them while on earth. They too will have eternal spiritual minds which will not be limited in the way their physical minds are now.

We have no grounds for believing that the differences between those who will be in *heaven* and those who will be in *hell*, will be in their *abilities* to think, to reason, to experience satisfaction and enjoyment. The differences will be in the *natures* of people which direct the way the abilities are used and in their different environments.

As people will share *hell* with Satan, the devil, it is instructive to learn the characteristics of the nature which he shares with all those with him. Three words summarise these characteristics. 'Pride' — expressed in the intention to be independent of his Creator, God: *"I will make myself like the Most High."* [1] 'Liar' — *"he is a liar and the father of it,"* [2] and 'deceiver' — *"as the serpent deceived Eve ..."* [3]

The 'separation' of God from people in *hell* will correspond to their desire to be independent of Him. Truth will be what people want it to be and the presentation of themselves will be of their own making.

During this life everyone, whether 'born again' Christians or not, has some knowledge of God's scheme of things for people — from their consciences, the law of Moses, evidence from the natural world, and the Bible. After the 'great divide', the 'righteous, forgiven sinners' will experience the fulfilment of all that God, in His grace, has promised. The 'unrighteous, unforgiven sinners', will experience the removal of all they have received of the 'grace of God' and rejected. Jesus spelled out this 'great divide':

"For to everyone who has will more be given, and he will have an abundance. But from the one who has not, even what he has will be taken away." [4]

The 'great divide' will separate:

(a) the environments — *heaven,* the destiny of the 'saints' or 'forgiven sinners', from — *hell* the destiny of the 'unholy' or 'unforgiven sinners';

(b) those with 'made righteous', godly natures' from those with 'unrighteous' ungodly natures.

A final word comes from Jesus, quoting Abraham:

"And besides all this, between us and you a great chasm has been fixed, in order that those who would pass from here to you may not do so, and none may cross from there to us." [5]

There could be no more complete divide.

---

[1] Isaiah 14:8 [2] John 8:44 [3] 2 Corinthians 11:3 [4] Matthew 25:29 [5] Luke 16:26

Chapter 8

The Harvest

The Apostle Paul warned the church in Galatia:
"Do not be deceived: God is not mocked, for whatever one sows, that will he also reap," [1]

He was repeating a principle that goes right through the Bible. Reaping is the inevitable consequence of sowing.

Jesus referred to the final event of history as we know it as the 'harvest' — the time to reap what has been sown. In our usual use of the term, harvests are the result of the efforts of cultivators. What the cultivator sows he reaps. Where the farmer sows wheat, if all goes well, he reaps a harvest of wheat. Certainly he will not harvest a crop of barley.

This kind of harvest is a picture of the spiritual harvest of which Jesus spoke in that the crop harvested depends on the seed sown. So it is with people. They will reap in the final eternal harvest what they have sown during their life on earth. That harvest will be reaped in their 'natural' or 'born again' natures and in the *environments* of either *hell* or *heaven*.

[1] Galatians 6:7

It remains to determine how the Bible describes that harvest, noting at the same time that the Bible records facts *from God's point of view*. When seen from an anti-God perspective, the facts are the same but the perception of them is different.

An important point, often missed, is that this spiritual harvest is composed of two parts:
- (a) that which will be imposed by God from *outside* a person in the environment of *heave*n or *hell*; and
- (b) that which will be from *within* a person as an expression of his or her nature.

The 'harvest' of the Christian — the 'forgiven sinner'
(a) From *outside* of themselves:

Christians who have trusted in Jesus and whose names are written in God's 'book of life' will be rewarded by the final removal from memory of all sins committed and forgiven during their lifetime on earth. God promised *"I will remember their sins no more."* [1] And they will receive rewards for what they did for Him, in His name, on earth and especially for the persecution many suffered and still suffer for His name.

The prophet Daniel was referring to this when he quoted God as saying:

"And those who are wise shall shine like the brightness of the sky above; and those who turn many to righteousness, like the stars for ever and ever." [2]

The Apostle Paul expanded on this:

"For no one can lay a foundation other than that which is laid, which is Jesus Christ. Now if anyone builds on the foundation with gold, silver, precious stones, wood, hay, straw — each one's work will become manifest, for the Day will disclose it, because it will be revealed by fire, and the fire will test what sort of work each one has done. If the work that anyone has built on the foundation survives, he will receive a reward." [3]

[1] Hebrews 8 12   [2] Daniel 12:3   [3] 1 Corinthians 3:11-14

The greater the faithfulness to Him in their lives, the greater will be the rewards. Jesus promised that even a friendly act to a seemingly undeserving person, done in His name, would be rewarded. Other pictures of rewards promised by Jesus occur in His parables:

"Well done, good and faithful servant. You have been faithful over a little; I will set you over much. Enter into the joy of your master." [1] *"Well done, good servant! Because you have been faithful in a very little, you shall have authority over ten cities."* [2]

Paul: *"if we endure, we will also reign with him ..."* [3]

And John: *"...and you have made them a kingdom and priests to our God, and they shall reign on the earth."* [4]

Whatever the final form of the rewards which God promises they are greatly to be desired by Christians.

(b) From *inside* themselves:

'Born again' Christians will carry into heaven the full enjoyment of all they have allowed God to do in their natures during their lives as Christians. They will be perfected in the sense that there will be no trace of all that in them 'fell short of the glory of God' in their lives on earth.

The writer of the letter to the Hebrews described the final perfected state of 'born again' Christians as:

"the assembly of the firstborn who are enrolled in heaven, and to God, the judge of all, and to the spirits of the righteous made perfect." [5]

A person's *'without God'* nature begins to be transformed into the final *'with God'* nature the moment he or she is 'born again' into His kingdom and the transformation continues throughout life on earth. God 'predestined', that is, pre-intended and designed every one of His children to be *"conformed to the image* (or model) *of his Son."* [6]

[1] Matthew 25:21 [2] Luke 19:17 [3] 2 Timothy 2:12 [4] Revelation 5:10
[5] Hebrews 12:23 [6] Romans 8:29

The Apostle Peter described the transforming process as becoming in nature like God:

"His divine power has granted to us all things that pertain to life and godliness, through the knowledge of him who called us to his own glory and excellence, by which he has granted to us his precious and very great promises, so that through them you may become partakers of the divine nature, having escaped from the corruption that is in the world because of sinful desire." [1]

It is probably of this inner experience that Paul wrote:

"What no eye has seen, nor ear heard, nor the heart of man imagined, what God has prepared for those who love him" [2]

Those who share in the 'divine nature' will find their fulfilment in the environment of heaven

The 'harvest' of non-Christians:

Those whose names are not in God's 'book of life', will also reap what they sowed in their lives in two ways:

(a) From *outside* of themselves:

God will inflict just punishment for all evil actions committed on earth. Two features are significant: the severity of the punishment will be proportional to the evil committed, and the punishment will come to an end when it is completed. God is just and all who have committed evil deeds and who have not been forgiven through faith in Jesus, will suffer the anger of God.

"Vengeance (retribution) *is mine, I will repay, ... It is a fearful thing to fall into the hands of the living God."* [3]

We leave the nature of that retribution and its severity to God, knowing that it will be appropriate to the evil committed, that it will come to an end and that everyone, including the evil doer, will recognise His justice in the punishment given.

[1] 2 Peter 1:3-4 [2] 1 Corinthians 2:9 [3] Hebrews 10:31

8 The Harvest

Jesus illustrated this in the parable of the servant who was forgiven his very large debt by his master but then went on not only to refuse to forgive his fellow servant a much smaller sum, but to insist on a prison sentence until all was paid. Expressing God's view of the situation, the master said:

"'You wicked servant! I forgave you all that debt because you pleaded with me. And should not you have had mercy on your fellow servant, as I had mercy on you?' And in anger his master delivered him to the jailers, until he should pay all his debt."

Note: 'until he should pay all his debt'. And Jesus added,
"So also my heavenly Father will do to every one of you, if you do not forgive your brother from your heart." [1]

The implication of this parable is that those who act in evil ways, will, in justice, be punished until they have 'fully paid their debt' as justly determined by God. That is the harvest imposed by God from outside the persons concerned.

(b) From *inside* themselves:

In hell, non-Christians, that is *unforgiven sinners*, will experience for ever all that their inner 'natural' natures desire in their futile thinking. These natures will be as they were carried over from their lives on earth but in the environment of *hell*, that is, without the restraining influence of God.

At this point it is important to note the language Jesus used in referring to the destiny of those who reject God's offer of mercy. He said:

"And if your hand causes you to sin, cut it off...
And if your foot causes you to sin, cut it off. ...
And if your eye causes you to sin, tear it out..."
Then, for all three examples,
"It is better for you to enter the kingdom of God with one eye (hand or foot) than with two eyes (hands or feet) to be

[1] Matthew 18:32-35

thrown into hell, where their worm does not die and the fire is not quenched." [2]

Hands, feet and eyes perform most of a person's most important functions. Two facts may be drawn from this statement of Jesus:

(a) The loss of any one of those parts of the body in this life is small compared to the gain of entering *heaven* rather than *hell*.

(b) The loss of enjoyment of the use of the equivalent of one hand, foot or eye in *heaven* will be as nothing compared to the torment that the equivalent of all those parts of the body will contribute to the torment of *hell*.

The term *hell* (gehenna) is derived from the Valley of Hinnom. This was the rubbish dump of those days. Into it were thrown everything which people wanted to get rid of including the bodies of those who died from leprosy. A fire burned continuously to consume the flammable material and worms consumed dead bodies of animals or people, and there was no stream passing through it to allow the growth of plants.

A significant point in the words of Jesus was His reference to *"their worm does not die and the fire is not quenched."* Both the *worm* and the *fire* in the Valley of Hinnom were self-perpetuating and not imposed from the outside.

The important facts which emerge from the words of Jesus and those later used by the Apostle John in Revelation, are that the experience of hell will be like:

(a) a fire which burns for ever,

(b) a thirst which is never quenched,

(c) a worm which never dies.

The word used to sum up these three areas of experience in hell is *torment*. Torture is physical suffering from some *outside* source, torment is mental and physical suffering from *inside* the person.

[1] Mark 9:43-49

Although there is no biblical analysis of this inner torment, it is possible to recognize five levels of severity:

(a) For those with *no 'light' — knowledge of truth*.

For the person who is, for whatever reason, unable to discern 'right from wrong' — babies who have died before reaching an age when their actions can be motivated morally and those who are mentally unable to grasp moral values to act on — for such, there will be no memory of acting against the 'light' available to them and hence no spiritual torment.

(b) For whom the 'light' is the *conscience*:

The Apostle Paul defined this level of 'light' when referring to non-Jews who did not have the law of Moses.

"For all who have sinned without the law will also perish without the law . ... For when Gentiles, who do not have the law, by nature do what the law requires, they are a law to themselves, even though they do not have the law. They show that the work of the law is written on their hearts, while their conscience also bears witness, and their conflicting thoughts accuse or even excuse them on that day when, according to my gospel, God judges the secrets of men by Christ Jesus." [1]

The evil doers of Sodom and Gomorrah did not have the law of Moses by which to judge their behaviour, but they had consciences which they flouted to gratify their desires.

Jude refers to the situation before the law was given:

"Just as Sodom and Gomorrah and the surrounding cities, which likewise indulged in sexual immorality and pursued unnatural desire, serve as an example by undergoing a punishment of eternal fire." [2]

The level of the torment will be related to the way people act relative to their consciences described here as *"their conflicting thoughts accuse or even excuse them"* on the day of God's judgement.

[1] Romans 2:12-16 [2] Jude 1:7

(c) For whom the 'light' is *the natural world*.

The Apostle Paul was forthright about the guilt of those who looked at the natural world with its vast evidence of design and then, in their futile thinking, rejected the Creator:

"For the wrath of God is revealed from heaven against all ungodliness and unrighteousness of men, who by their unrighteousness suppress the truth. For what can be known about God is plain to them, because God has shown it to them. For his invisible attributes, namely, his eternal power and divine nature, have been clearly perceived, ever since the creation of the world, in the things that have been made. So they are without excuse. For although they knew God, they did not honour him as God or give thanks to him, but they became futile in their thinking, and their foolish hearts were darkened. Claiming to be wise, they became fools, and exchanged the glory of the immortal God for images resembling mortal man and birds and animals and creeping things." [1]

The torment of those whose 'light' is nature's clear evidence of a Creator-God will be the memory of rejecting Him as creator, preferring to worship idols of their own making and inventing futile philosophies. This rejection of the logical conclusion of observing the universe is 'suppressing the truth' for themselves and for those they influence.

(d) For whom the 'light' is the *law as revealed to Moses*:

To quote Paul again,

"... all who have sinned under the law will be judged by the law." [2]

Clearly those who act in disobedience to the 'light' of the known law of God through Moses, will experience greater 'torment' as they remember rejecting God's will to pursue their own. Jesus made this clear when briefing His disciples for their preaching tour:

[1] Romans 1:18-25 [2] Romans 2:12

"And if anyone will not receive you or listen to your words, shake off the dust from your feet when you leave that house or town. Truly, I say to you, it will be more bearable on the day of judgment for the land of Sodom and Gomorrah than for that town." [1]

On another occasion, Jesus spelled out the same message but referred to specific places:

"Woe to you, Chorazin! Woe to you, Bethsaida! For if the mighty works done in you had been done in Tyre and Sidon, they would have repented long ago in sackcloth and ashes. But I tell you, it will be more bearable on the day of judgment for Tyre and Sidon than for you. And you, Capernaum, will you be exalted to heaven? You will be brought down to Hades. For if the mighty works done in you had been done in Sodom, it would have remained until this day. But I tell you that it will be more tolerable on the day of judgment for the land of Sodom than for you." [2]

The law of God revealed through Moses is not a set of arbitrary rules to govern society. To reject that law is to rebel against God and His order for society.

(e) For whom the 'light' is *God's grace as revealed in Jesus Christ*:

The law revealed through Moses was a great step forward in understanding the kind of social order for which God created people. An even greater step was revealed when Jesus came to live as God and Man on earth, to teach explicitly of what the 'kingdom of heaven' was like.

The Apostle John stated this in one sentence:

"For the law was given through Moses; grace and truth came through Jesus Christ." [3]

The writer of the letter to the Hebrews compared the situation as it applied to them then:

[1] Matthew 10:14-16 [2] Matthew 11:22-25 [3] John 1:17

"Anyone who has set aside the law of Moses dies without mercy on the evidence of two or three witnesses." [1]

Then, referring to life after death:

"How much worse punishment, do you think, will be deserved by the one who has spurned the Son of God, and has profaned the blood of the covenant by which he was sanctified, and has outraged the Spirit of grace? ... It is a fearful thing to fall into the hands of the living God." [2]

Elsewhere, the same writer spelled out the same message even more strongly.

"For it is impossible, in the case of those who have once been enlightened, who have tasted the heavenly gift, and have shared in the Holy Spirit, and have tasted the goodness of the word of God and the powers of the age to come, and then have fallen away, to restore them again to repentance, since they are crucifying once again the Son of God to their own harm and holding him up to contempt." [3]

The Apostle Peter expressed this very vividly in the passage already quoted:

"For if, after they have escaped the defilements of the world through the knowledge of our Lord and Savior Jesus Christ, they are again entangled in them and overcome, the last state has become worse for them than the first. For it would have been better for them never to have known the way of righteousness than after knowing it to turn back from the holy commandment delivered to them." [4]

These warnings are stern indeed. Those who have 'tasted the goodness of God' — read the Bible, seen the effects of His life in others and have benefited from His influence in the world —and then, for their own self-centred interests or through placing their futile thinking above that of His word — e.g. liberal theology — have rejected His offer of mercy, the severity of their torment will be great indeed.

[1] Hebrews 10:28-31 [2] Hebrews 10:29-31 [3] Hebrews 6:4-8 [4] 2 Peter 2:20-22

(f) For those who spend their time in futile activities.

Jesus said:

"I tell you, on the day of judgment people will give account for every careless word they speak." [1]

The writer to the Hebrews confirmed this:

"And no creature is hidden from his sight, but all are naked and exposed to the eyes of him to whom we must give account." [2]

Futile thinking is a sign of not living in the real spiritual world. It can be wasting precious time in spiritually futile or unproductive activities rather than in fulfilling God's purposes. It can be living in the world of the imagination.

(g) For those who withhold from others the 'light' of God's grace.

It was not often that Jesus pronounced a 'woe' to an evil doer but probably the most severe was to those who were obstacles to others learning God's truth for them:

"Whoever receives one such child in my name receives me, but whoever causes one of these little ones who believe in me to sin, it would be better for him to have a great millstone fastened around his neck and to be drowned in the depth of the sea." [3]

Jesus made this point very strongly when addressing some Jewish religious leaders:

"Woe to you, scribes and Pharisees, hypocrites! For you travel across sea and land to make a single proselyte, and when he becomes a proselyte, you make him twice as much a child of hell as yourselves." [4]

It seems likely that the torment of those who have led others astray will be made worse by the presence with them in *hell*, of those whom they have influenced against God or have prevented or hindered from trusting in Him.

---

[1] Matthew 12:36 [2] Hebrews 4:13 [3] Matthew 18:5-6 [4] Matthew 23:15

To summarize:

The 'harvest' for 'forgiven sinners' will be the *outward* rewards God gives for faithfulness in service for Him or for others in His name, and the *inner* experience of living with their natures made perfect by the final obliteration from memory of all that, in their lifetime on earth, fell short of God's perfect holiness and for which they were forgiven through trusting in Jesus, and the eternal joy of 'natures made perfect', in the 'total moral light' of the environment of *heaven*.

The 'harvest' for 'unforgiven sinners' will be the *outward* punishment imposed on them for the evil acts they have committed in this life, punishment which will end when completed, and the *inner* torment of living for ever with themselves as their spiritual natures were formed by the actions they chose to perform in their lives on earth, to be experienced in the environment of 'utter moral darkness' which will be *hell*.

Chapter 9

Enjoyment and torment

The experiences of enjoyment and torment are illustrated by incidents in both the Old and New Testaments:

Lot in Sodom
Writing of the destruction of Sodom and Gomorrah, the Apostle Peter wrote:
*"For if God did not spare angels when they sinned, but cast them into hell and committed them to chains of gloomy darkness to be kept until the judgment; ... if by turning the cities of Sodom and Gomorrah to ashes he condemned them to extinction, making them an example of what is going to happen to the ungodly; and if he rescued righteous Lot, greatly distressed by the sensual conduct of the wicked (for as that righteous man lived among them day after day, he was **tormenting** his righteous soul over their lawless deeds that he saw and heard); then the Lord knows how to rescue the godly from trials, and to keep the unrighteous under punishment until the day of judgment, and especially those who indulge in the lust of defiling passion and despise authority."* [1]

---
[1] 2 Peter 2:4-10

The Rich man and Lazarus

The story Jesus told of the rich man and Lazarus is the only description we are given of life after death and before the final judgement. It is worth reading in full.

*"There was a rich man who was clothed in purple and fine linen and who feasted sumptuously every day. And at his gate was laid a poor man named Lazarus, covered with sores, who desired to be fed with what fell from the rich man's table. Moreover, even the dogs came and licked his sores. The poor man died and was carried by the angels to Abraham's side. The rich man also died and was buried, and in Hades, being in **torment**, he lifted up his eyes and saw Abraham far off and Lazarus at his side. And he called out, 'Father Abraham, have mercy on me, and send Lazarus to dip the end of his finger in water and cool my tongue, for I am in **anguish** in this flame. But Abraham said, 'Child, remember that you in your lifetime received good things, and Lazarus in like manner bad things; but now he is comforted here and you in **anguish.**'"* [1]

The rich man enjoyed his greed during his lifetime while Lazarus suffered. In *Hades — the place of the dead,* and later *hell*, the situation is reversed. Lazarus is comforted while the 'rich man' is in torment. The fact that the rich man wanted to save his brothers from his fate suggests that he retained a strong memory of the past. He must have realized that he, as well as his brothers, knew the teaching of 'Moses and the prophets' and had rejected or ignored it. They enjoyed their lifestyle while alive on earth. The testimony of someone who claimed to have come to life again would not make them change their minds or their behaviour.

"If they do not hear Moses and the prophets, neither will they be convinced if someone should rise from the dead." [2]

[1] Luke 16:19-25 [2] Luke 16:31

9 Enjoyment and torment

It is noteworthy that both Lot and the 'rich man' to whom Jesus refers were in *torment, agony* or *anguish*. Different versions of the Bible use all these terms. The difference is that Lot's torment was of a *righteous* man in an *unrighteous* environment, while the 'rich man's' torment was of an *unrighteous* man in a *righteous* environment. While they were alive on earth, Lot was *tormented* by the evil pleasure he saw around him while the rich man took *pleasure* in the evil inequality he enjoyed.

The fact that, from Hades, Lazarus
"... lift up his eyes, being in torments, and saw Abraham afar off, and Lazarus in his bosom," [1]
suggests strongly that he, Lazarus, was aware of the environment of paradise from where he was *"far off"*. The use of the term 'bosom' is very significant. According to W E Vine it is used figuratively for 'a place of blessedness with another'. A baby at a mother's breast comes to mind.

Lazarus was in such a place. The 'rich man' was not.

Each of the incidents quoted refer to the points of view of those who were experiencing different situations. The activities of the people of Sodom and Gomorrah were, for them, *enjoyable*. Those activities were the natural expressions of their natural natures which gave them pleasure. From Lot's point of view, however, those activities were contrary to his nature. They were evil and abhorrent. What was *torment* to 'righteous Lot' was *enjoyment* to the unrighteous people of Sodom and Gomorrah.

In the story of the rich man and Lazarus, it was the 'rich man' who was *tormented* while Lazarus *enjoyed* the intimacy of the presence of God. In the environment of Hades, a prelude to hell, the rich pleaded for water *"for I am in anguish in this flame."* [2]

[1] Luke 16:23 KJV [2] Luke 16:24

In response Jesus quoted Abraham:

"Child, remember that you in your lifetime received good things, and Lazarus in like manner bad things; but now he is comforted here and you in anguish."

In the Bible, fire means two things:

(a) in the hands of a skilled artisan it is a means of refining coarse ores in order to produce the pure metal, and

(b) it is the means of destroying that which is evil, as in Genesis:

"Then the Lord rained on Sodom and Gomorrah sulphur and fire from the Lord out of heaven." [1]

In the Bible, *water* is used to convey the idea of 'giving life' to that which is dead. Jesus said of the water in the well by which he was sitting:

"Everyone who drinks of this water will be thirsty again. but whoever drinks of the water that I will give him will never be thirsty again. The water that I will give him will become in him a spring of water welling up to eternal life." [2]

In heaven there will be water and all that it means of life-giving:

"Then the angel showed me the river of the water of life, bright as crystal, flowing from the throne of God" [3]

But there will be no destructive fire. The 'refining fire' of which the Bible speaks will have achieved its purpose.

In hell, there will be the destruction represented by *fire*, but no life-giving in the sense represented by *water*. The 'fire of hell' will be people's experience of the destruction caused by the removal of all that is good and holy received from God's influence in this life, as He 'gives them up' to their own self-centred desires. Whatever maybe the full spiritual significance of water, there will be none of it in hell. But of all that fire represents spiritually? Yes!

[1] Genesis 19:24 [2] John 4:13-14 [3] Revelation 22:1

9 Enjoyment and torment

Dogs and pigs 'loving it'!

The Apostle Peter wrote to Christians alerting them of the deceptive tactics of false prophets in the past which would be repeated with even greater effect in the future.

False teachers will introduce destructive heresies which will deceive many. Referring to those who, although having experienced life in a Christian setting, follow false teachers and reject their faith, he wrote:

"For if, after they have escaped the defilements of the world through the knowledge of our Lord and Saviour Jesus Christ, they are again entangled in them and overcome, the last state has become worse for them than the first. For it would have been better for them never to have known the way of righteousness than after knowing it to turn back from the holy commandment delivered to them. What the true proverb says has happened to them, 'The dog returns to it's own vomit, and the sow, after washing herself, returns to wallow in the mire.'" [1]

The proverbs quoted by Peter are significant. The dog and the sow are washed clean. Surely they would be happy in that state! But no! They prefer their natural filthy state to the, for them, unnatural state of cleanness. They are quite happy to 'lick their vomit' and enjoy 'wallowing in the mire', however much the owner might consider these activities to be filthy and hateful.

Those who, in this life, understand what it is to be made spiritually clean by Jesus can be likened to the dog and the sow who have been washed by their owners in order to give them a better life. Those who then reject being made spiritually clean by God and return to their former ways are like the dog which *"returns to it's own vomit"* and the sow which *"returns to wallow in the mire."*

[1] 2 Peter 2:20-22

9 Enjoyment and torment

As the dog prefers and *enjoys* its vomit, and the sow *delights* in wallowing in the mire, so those in hell will be *happy* in satisfying the natural desires of their natural selves rather than, for them, the unnatural desires of a God-like nature.

The proverbs of the dog and the sow cannot be pressed too far. Neither of them have a mental and spiritual consciousness which would enable them to work out what they were doing and judge its consequences. They cannot understand the source of their desires nor of their actions ...

... *people can*!

We know what we are doing and are able to understand the consequences of our actions. We can, in this life, choose what we want to experience as *enjoyment* or *torment* in the environment of this life and so be prepared for the experiences that these terms describe in the life to come.

The experiences of Lot in Sodom and Gomorrah and of the rich man and Lazarus are replicated today. Many children appear to enjoy bullying other children for whom such activity is torment. Many Christians in the world experience the torment of persecution as the perpetrators take delight in inflicting pain and even death on those they detest. There are well-known and popular films which depict the amusement some gain from inflicting grievous pain. Usually, however, in the interests of law and order, the 'goodies' usually win over the 'baddies'.

It is universally true that one man's *enjoyment* is another man's *torment*.

And vice versa!

Chapter 10

The symbolism of heaven and hell

A symbol is a thing, a mark, a character or sign that represents something else. The symbolism of *heaven* and *hell* is a series of objects or situations which represent spiritual things or situations.

The most universally recognized Christian symbol is the Cross. The wooden cross on which Jesus was crucified was a material object, but it represents what happened at the most important event in history. Many books have been written to explain that symbolism.

As it is important to understand the symbolism of the Cross in order to understand the significance of what was achieved by the act it represents, so it is important to understand the symbolism of *heaven* and *hell* in order to understand the events or situations they represent.

An important principle in seeking this understanding is to recognize that the meanings of the symbols must be found in the context of the whole Bible, not in any one person's imagination nor in today's usage in any modern language.

10 The symbolism of heaven and hell

The new heaven and the new earth.
"Then I saw a new heaven and a new earth, for the first heaven and the first earth had passed away and the sea was no more." [1]

'Heaven', 'earth' and 'sea' are all used as symbols drawn from the physical environment in which we live now. 'Heaven' or 'heavens' here means the atmosphere which surrounds the earth and includes outer space with its galaxies of stars. Other biblical references give us clues to an understanding of the 'new heaven and the new earth'.

"I create new heavens and a new earth and the former things (troubles) *shall not be remembered or come into mind."* [2] *"For as the new heavens and the new earth that I make shall remain before me, says the LORD, shall your offspring and your name remain."* [3] *"But according to his promise we are waiting for new heavens and a new earth in which righteousness dwells."* [4]

From these passages we can discern the meanings of the symbolism. The 'new heaven and the new earth' will be where people live after life in the present 'heaven (sky) and earth' is ended. The land masses of this earth are separated by seas. There will be no such separation in heaven.

That the future 'heaven' is described in terms of the present 'heaven' or 'heavens' means that, although very different, there will be a continuity of ideas between them. The phrase 'world without end', which occurs several times in the Bible, implies a continuity that is not fully explained.

The revelation given to John completes the picture by underlining heaven's chief characteristic — a moral one.

"... nothing unclean will ever it, nor anyone who does what is detestable or false." [5]

A precise description of the future 'new heaven and new earth' is beyond our present human powers to understand.

[1] Revelation 21:1 [2] Isaiah 65:17 [3] Isaiah 66:22-23 [4] 2 Peter 3:13 [5] Revelation 21:27

The new Jerusalem

"And I saw the holy city, the new Jerusalem, coming down out of heaven from God, prepared as a bride adorned for her husband. And I heard a loud voice from the throne saying, 'Behold, the dwelling place of God is with man. He will dwell with them, and they will be his people and God himself will be with them as their God.'" [1]

The symbolic language —'the holy city', 'the new Jerusalem', the 'bride adorned for her husband'— refers to both a future situation and to a very significant event which will take place in 'the new heavens and the new earth'.

Cities are frequently mentioned in the Bible. They are:

(a) Places where people live in close proximity to each other as compared to those who live in country areas. In heaven, everyone will be in easy reach of each other.

(b) The centres of government and all forms of authority. The present Jerusalem is the city which God has chosen as the place associated with His name as contrasted with Babylon, the city associated with His adversary, the Devil. 'The bride' is a very meaningful symbol of the relationship of people to God in the New Jerusalem. It was of the church as the 'bride of Christ' that he wrote:

Husbands, love your wives, as Christ loved the church" [2]

John's vision was of a feast:

"Let us rejoice and exult and give him the glory, for the marriage of the Lamb has come, and his Bride has made herself ready." [3]

The 'new Jerusalem' will be accessible to everyone in heaven. It will be the seat of government of God's 'heavenly kingdom', the centre of the new universe — 'the new heavens and the new earth', and the permanent home of the Family of God: God the Father, God the Son, Jesus and His bride, the church, and God the Holy Spirit.

[1] Revelation 21:2 [2] Ephesians 5 25 [3] Revelation 19:7

The lake of fire and brimstone

The Apostle John links the 'lake of fire and brimstone' with the 'second death' — the final separation from God

"But the cowardly, unbelieving, abominable, murderers, sexually immoral, sorcerers, idolaters, and all liars shall have their part in the lake which burns with fire and brimstone, which is the second death." [1]

The first reference to 'brimstone' appears in the destruction of the two evil cities where Lot lived:

"Then the LORD rained upon Sodom and upon Gomorrah brimstone and fire from the LORD out of heaven." [2]

Moses warned the children of Israel while in the desert against 'turning away from God' by referring to the places where people had so acted:

"The whole land burned out with brimstone and salt, nothing sown and nothing growing, where no plant can sprout, an overthrow like that of Sodom and Gomorrah, Admah, and Zeboiim, which the LORD overthrew in his anger and wrath" [3]

Those who tried to counsel Job pointed to what they considered happens to the wicked man:

"He is up-rooted from the shelter of his tent ... brimstone is scattered on his dwelling ... the memory of him perishes from the earth." [4]

God, through Isaiah, prophesied of God's judgement:

"For it is the day of the Lord's vengeance ... its streams shall be turned into pitch and its dust into brimstone ... from generation to generation it shall lie waste; no one shall pass through it for ever." [5]

The symbol of the 'lake of fire and brimstone' is that of a state of utter and permanent elimination from all that is of God, even from the memory of it, as judgement for rejecting Him and His purposes for the people in the lake.

[1] Revelation 21:8 KJV [2] Genesis 19:24 KJV [3] Deuteronomy 29:23
[4] Job 18:15 KJV [5] Isaiah 34:9 KJV

The 'worm that will not die' and 'the fire which will not be quenched'.

The word 'worm' is used in two senses in the Bible. The first refers to the worm as the meanest of animal life. *"I am a worm and not a man,"* [1] wrote King David.

The second sense forms the context of the words of Jesus when referring to hell: *"where their worm does not die and the fire is not quenched."* [2]

Quoting God, Isaiah wrote:

"Listen to me, you who know righteousness, the people in whose heart is my law; fear not the reproach of man, nor be dismayed at their revilings. For the moth will eat them up like a garment, and the worm will eat them like wool; but my righteousness will be forever, and my salvation to all generations." [3]

In the passage already quoted, Isaiah prophesied of the last great battle:

"And they shall go out and look on the dead bodies of the men who have rebelled against me. For their worm shall not die, their fire shall not be quenched, and they shall be an abhorrence to all flesh." [4]

In referring to *"their worm shall not die"* and *"their fire shall not be quenched"*, Jesus was speaking to people to whom the prophecy of Isaiah was known and was quite understandable. For the Jews of that period, these terms would be associated with the Valley of Hinnom as already mentioned on page 52.

The significant point about this valley was that the fire which burned up the flammable rubbish and the worms which consumed all forms of dead flesh — animal and human — continued without the fire having to be relit and more worms introduced. They were self perpetuating from within their situations.

[1] Psalm 22:6 [2] Mark 9:48 [3] Isaiah 51:8 [4] Isaiah 66:24

As the term *hell* (gehenna) is derived from the Valley of Hinnom, the symbolism of *'the worm never dies"* and *"the fire which never dies out'*, expresses the never-ending of the spiritual torment in *hell* which is the product from within of the 'natural' nature of the people there. This will probably include the mental suffering caused by the memory of what might have been had they acted differently on earth.

The 'river of life' and 'the tree of life'.

In the vision of heaven God gave John:

"Then the angel showed me the river of the water of life, bright as crystal, flowing from the throne of God and of the Lamb through the middle of the street of the city; also, on either side of the river, the tree of life with its twelve kinds of fruit, yielding its fruit each month. The leaves of the tree were for the healing of the nations." [1]

Jesus explained the meaning of the 'river of life' when he said to the Samaritan woman He met at the well:

"Jesus said to her, 'Everyone who drinks of this water will be thirsty again, but whoever drinks of the water that I will give him will never be thirsty again. The water that I will give him will become in him a spring of water welling up to eternal life.'" [2]

For the meaning of the symbolism of the 'tree of life' it is necessary to go back to the Genesis record of creation and the events which immediately followed it. The first act of God after bringing into being 'the heavens and the earth' and all forms of life, was to 'plant a garden':

"And out of the ground the LORD God made to spring up every tree that is pleasant to the sight and good for food. The tree of life was in the midst of the garden, and the tree of the knowledge of good and evil." [3]

"Then the LORD God said, 'Behold, the man has become like one of us in knowing good and evil. Now, lest he reach

[1] Revelation 22:1-2   [2] John 4:13-14   [3] Genesis 2:9

out his hand and take also of the tree of life and eat, and live forever—' therefore the LORD God sent him out from the garden of Eden to work the ground from which he was taken." [1]

Centuries later, Jesus referred to that tree.

"To the one who conquers I will grant to eat of the tree of life which is in the paradise of God." [2]

The significance of the symbol 'the tree of life' is undoubtedly that of 'eternal life' — everyone who ate of the tree would live for ever. It is more difficult to work out the meaning of the *"twelve kinds of fruit, yielding its fruit each month. The leaves of the tree were for the healing of the nations."*

Light and darkness

In John's vision of the New Jerusalem:

"And the city has no need of sun or moon to shine on it, for the glory of God gives it light, and its lamp is the Lamb. By its light will the nations walk, and the kings of the earth will bring their glory into it, and its gates will never be shut by day—and there will be no night there." [3]

Jesus gives us the meaning of the symbol of light

"Again Jesus spoke to them, saying, "I am the light of the world. Whoever follows me will not walk in darkness, but will have the light of life." [4]

The symbols of 'light' and 'darkness' are defined in terms of the presence or absence of God. In this life, those in whom God is living have 'spiritual light' and those who are separated from God are in 'spiritual darkness'.

Light and darkness are symbols of both what is true and what is false, and what is real and what is imaginary

"God is light, and in him is no darkness at all. If we say we have fellowship with him while we walk in darkness, we lie and do not practice the truth. But if we walk in the light,

---

[1] Genesis 3:22-23 [2] Revelation 2:7 [3] Revelation 21:23-25 [4] John 8:12

as he is in the light, we have fellowship with one another, and the blood of Jesus his Son cleanses us from all sin. If we say we have no sin, we deceive ourselves, and the truth is not in us." [1]

'Light' and 'darkness' are to be understood in two senses:

(a) 'light' is truth where 'darkness' is lies, deceit:

(b) 'light' is reality, genuineness, where 'darkness' is unreality, imagination, falsity, futility.

Heaven will be 'total light — total truth and reality — with no darkness — no falsity or unreality — at all'.

Hell will be where there is 'outer darkness' — truth made to fit, and virtual reality the norm.

Throughout the Bible, symbolism is used to refer to the spirit world in terms drawn from the physical world in which we live. According to our natural understanding, the physical world is solid—visible, tangible, whereas the spirit world is, to our present way of thinking, abstract — invisible, intangible. For us now, it is the physical world which appears to be real and the spirit world unreal. In the *heaven* and *hell* to come it will be the spirit environment which is real and the environment of the earth a memory.

---

[1] 1 John 1:5-8

Chapter 11

The two points of view

It is now possible to discern the differences in the points of view of God, and hence, of those who have the 'nature of God', and of those who do not.

Heaven — As seen by 'children of God'
Life in heaven will be beyond anything we can fully imagine in this life. Understood from God's point of view, life will be characterized by the full enjoyment of eternal, perfect 'light'—openness between God and each other, and 'love'—total commitment to God and to each other. Whatever the activities may be, relationships between God and every one else will be perfectly enjoyable.

Jesus referred to heaven when He answered a question about the situation of those who have married more than once:

"The sons of this age marry and are given in marriage, but those who are considered worthy to attain to that age and to the resurrection from the dead neither marry nor are given in marriage, for they cannot die anymore, because they are equal to angels and are sons of God, being sons of the resurrection." [1]

[1] Luke 20:34-36

11 The two points of view

Reference has already been made to Daniel's prophecy that at the resurrection from the dead some will wake to
"everlasting life ... and those who are wise shall shine like the brightness of the sky above and those who turn many to righteousness, like the stars for ever and ever." [1]

Our understanding of what heaven will be like, from the Christian's point of view, depends on what we understand of Jesus. In the words of the Apostle John:
"Beloved, we are God's children now, and what we will be has not yet appeared; but we know that when he appears we shall be like him, because we shall see him as he is." [2]

This was spelled out by the Apostle Paul:
"What no eye has seen, nor ear heard, nor the heart of man imagined, what God has prepared for those who love him." [3]

Those 'made righteous' will, in heaven, be in the 'bosom of the Father', a place of 'perfect blessedness'. The present universe was and is corrupted by the rebellion of 'unrighteous' men and women. In the heaven to come:
"But nothing unclean will ever enter it, nor anyone who does what is detestable or false, but only those who are written in the Lamb's book of life." [4]

Heaven, as viewed by those who are children of God, will be a place of total 'blessedness' without anything that has corrupted life on the earth as it is now.

Heaven — As seen by those who are not 'children of God'

Seen from the point of view of those who, in their life on earth, have delighted in their self-centred ways at the expense of other people, who have enjoyed deceiving people and delighted in presenting themselves in false and hypocritical ways, and who have been happy to live without

[2] Daniel 12:2-3 [2] 1 John 3:1-3 [3] 1 Corinthians 2:9 [4] Revelation 21:27

reference to their Creator-God, the heaven environment would be very uncomfortable and unpleasant. Millions of people live as though the known existence and presence of their Creator-God among them would be an obstacle to gaining all they desire. They are quite happy without Him.

The openness of relationships in heaven which, for the 'righteous' with nothing to hide, will be a delight, would be for the 'unrighteous' an intrusion, an uncovering of what they want to hide and a limit to their enjoyment.

Hell — As seen by those who are 'children of God'

Seen from God's point of view, life in hell would be like an *'inextinguishable fire'* — burning up every God-given desire and loving intention. It would be like an *'unquenchable thirst'* — for real, loving relationships and genuine love-motivated goals to attain. It would be like a *'worm which will not die'* — undying memory of the times in their lives when they experienced a different environment.

It is this view of hell which is presented in the Bible and it is fearsome indeed. Everyone who responds to God's influence on them in this life and 'loves the light' He gives them, will view the conditions of the 'outer darkness' of *hell* with dread indeed.

Hell —As seen by those who are not 'children of God'

There is no doubt that those who have committed evil against God and against other people will experience from Him a just punishment for their actions. The severity of this punishment will be proportional to the gravity of the evil actions committed. This punishment will reflect the anger or wrath of God towards those who have twisted His word and behaved in evil ways despite having known the 'light' He gave them through their consciences, the law of Moses and the sacrifice of Jesus for them. This part of hell will be seen as being cast into a 'lake of fire and brimstone' until, metaphorically speaking, the fire has destroyed the evil committed. They will not enjoy that experience!

The eternal 'torment' of hell is different in that it will be for ever, and it will come from *within* people's natures and will depend on their actions and their futile thinking relative to the 'light' available to them — their consciences, the evidence of the natural world, the law given through Moses, or a knowledge of the Gospel. Apart from the punishment for evil committed and the memory of, for some at least, what might have been had they acted differently, the view of hell will not be at all unenjoyable.

For those who have put self-centred interests and futile or vain thinking above all other considerations in this life, the environment of hell will be attractive. There will be there all the very best that virtual reality can offer, with no possibility of hurting anyone else physically.

There is one passage in the Bible in which Jesus suggests that there will be a limited measure of good in the final environment of hell:

"If you love those who love you, what benefit is that to you? For even sinners love those who love them. And if you do good to those who do good to you, what benefit is that to you? For even sinners do the same. And if you lend to those from whom you expect to receive, what credit is that to you? Even sinners lend to sinners, to get back the same amount" [1]

If, in this life, the 'sinners' find it in themselves to love those who love them — a selfish 'love', and do good to those who do good to them and lend to those who will give them interest on their loans, it is logical to imagine that these kinds of actions will be repeated by 'sinners' in *hell*. Note that in each case, the action towards another is the expression of a self-centred nature working for its own ends.

[1] Luke 6:32-34

11 The two points of view

If, as the Bible confirms, people now — *"delight in their abominations"*, *"love evil more than good and lying more than speaking what is right"*, *"love vain words and seek after lies"*, *"bless with their mouths but inwardly they curse"*, *"delight in war"*, *"rejoice in doing evil and delight in the perverseness of evil"*, approve and applaud others who practice ... every kind of unrighteousness", *"count it pleasure to revel in the daytime ... revelling in their deceptions"*, are *"lovers of pleasure rather than lovers of God"* — then in *hell*, when God gives them up to their own desires, they will surely delight in their freedom from Him and from all restraints imposed by Him in this present life. Their natures, without all that is good from God, will have desires very different from those who 'share in the divine nature'.

An indication of the extent of this freedom can be found in the behaviour of people when faced with opportunities to pursue their ends but are limited by social conditions. Situations where law and order break down provide ample evidence of what people would do if there were no restrictions. Stealing is a common practice when there is no one to observe the action. Fear of being found out is a serious deterrent. The moral value of an action — whether it is right or wrong — is seen by many people to depend on the situation rather than on the nature of the act.

A personal experience illustrates this. When, in the 1960s, I was seeking to help those whose houses were being burnt and were being forced to flee in Rwanda, Africa, I expressed my revulsion that a certain man had been killed because of his ethnicity. I was informed that his ethnicity had nothing to do with it. He was killed by someone who hated him and there was no enforcement of law to prevent it! For such, the environment of *no* law or order means *freedom* to act as desired.

The eagle and the pig

The two different points of view can be illustrated by comparing the situation of an eagle enjoying the freedom of flying in the bright expanse of the sky with that of a pig enjoying the freedom of wallowing in the mire in the darkness of the valley. Both enjoy freedom. The difference lies in the nature of their freedom and in the environments in which that freedom is exercised. Both the eagle and the pig enjoy doing what comes naturally to their natures.

If the eagle and the pig had consciousness as human beings have, the eagle would find the environment enjoyed by the pig to be *torment* indeed. For the pig, the environment of the eagle would not be at all desirable, in fact, contrary to its nature, except to the extent that it had, at some time in its life, been transported to a high mountain and shared to a limited extent the point of view of the eagle and found some aspects of it desirable.

So it will be in the final destinies of people. For the 'righteous', *hell* would be intolerable. For the 'unrighteous', *heaven* will not be at all desirable except for those who, in their lifetime, have caught a glimpse of heaven in a loving church environment or caring hospital, have rejected it and are tormented by what they have missed.

The big difference between the illustration and reality is that neither the eagle nor the pig have any choice.

People do!

The 'healthy' and 'unhealthy' eye.

Jesus illustrated the 'two views': *"The eye is the lamp of the body. So, if your eye is healthy, your whole body will be full of light, but if your eye is bad, your whole body will be full of darkness. If then the light in you is darkness, how great is the darkness!"* [1]

[1] Matthew 6:22-23

The spiritual nature of a person relative to his or her 'world view' that is, his or her point of view on spiritual matters, is like the "human eye' relative to the 'human body'. Whether or not the body is 'full of light' or 'full of darkness' depends on the health or soundness of the eye. The word translated 'healthy' means 'good', 'generous' and 'unself-centred'. The word translated 'bad' or 'unhealthy' means 'stingy' or self-centred. The 'eye' represents the nature of a person. If the nature is healthy, the outlook of the person is 'full of light'; if it is unhealthy, it is 'full of darkness'.

The nature of ungodly people, being 'full of darkness' will mean that they enjoy different things and see things differently from those whose nature is godly and therefore 'full of light'.

The two masters.

Jesus underlined the fact that no one has 'dual vision':

"No one can serve two masters, for either he will hate the one and love the other, or he will be devoted to the one and despise the other. You cannot serve God and money." [1]

Jesus also said:

"Do not lay up for yourselves treasures on earth, where moth and rust destroy and where thieves break in and steal, but lay up for yourselves treasures in heaven, where neither moth nor rust destroys and where thieves do not break in and steal. For where your treasure is there your heart will be also." [2]

The teaching of Jesus is simple. What a person does in this life is an investment into life after death. Whether they realize it or not, every one is laying up 'treasure' in this life for the next. Our natures determine our objectives, that is, the 'treasure' we lay up for ourselves. The 'treasure' is an expression of our point of view of what is, or is not worth living for.

[1] Matthew 6:24 [2] Matthew 6:19-21

11 The two points of view

In His parable of the dishonest manager, Jesus concluded:

"For the sons of this world are more shrewd in dealing with their own generation than the sons of light." [1]

Here Jesus refers to the 'unrighteous' as 'sons of this world' and those 'made righteous' as the 'sons of the light'. Different names but the same two different categories of people with different objectives in life. It follows that they will observe their situations from two different points of view.

Confirmation came from Jesus Himself:

"The Pharisees, who were lovers of money, heard all these things, and they ridiculed him. And he said to them, 'You are those who justify yourselves before men, but God knows your hearts. For what is exalted among men is an abomination in the sight of God.'" [2]

The teaching of Jesus is clear:

"If your eye is healthy, your whole body will be full of light, but if your eye is unhealthy, your whole body will be full of darkness." "No one can serve two masters". "Where your treasure is there your heart will be also." "For what is exalted among men is an abomination in the sight of God."

A person's nature determines his or her point of view.

Metaphorically speaking, what to one person is 'white' is, to another person, 'black'.

And vice versa.

---

[1] Luke 16:8 [2] Luke 16:14-15

Chapter 12

Conclusion

We return to the problems which many Christians face when thinking about *heaven* and *hell*:

The presentation of:

(a) *Hell* as a state of unimaginable and everlasting pain and torment for *'unrepentant sinners'*, to be viewed with utmost fear and horror.

(b) *Heaven* which God enjoys with the 'saints'— *the 'forgiven sinners'*, knowing that, in *hell*, everyone else — *the unforgiven sinners* — are enduring unending torment.

This problem of the uncomfortable combination of ideas: *hell* and the *God of love*, can now be resolved.

The underlying principle which make this resolution possible is the recognition that:

(a) The final destinies of *heaven* and *hell* are presented in the Bible from *God's point of view*.

(b) This point of view is an expression of God's nature. It will be shared only by those whose minds He enlightens or who share His nature. Those whose minds are not enlightened by Him or do not share His nature will see *heaven* and *hell* differently.

12 Conclusion

We apply these principles to the biblical presentations of *heaven* and *hell*. In the life after death, there will be two groups of people *enjoying* themselves as they satisfy their different natures in their different environments. Everyone will be, in differing measures, *content*. The differences will be in the *nature of their contentment* and the *environment* in which it is experienced.

Seen from God's point of view, for 'godly' people, who share the 'divine nature', the environment of *hell* will be unbearably and unimaginably appalling, and in stark contrast to the joys of heaven. However, as viewed by those who do not share God's nature and are not enlightened by Him, who, in this life have lived their lives happily without Him and have enjoyed following their own self-centred desires, the prospect of hell will not be at all daunting. After God's punishment for the evil they have committed, the only obstacle to the full enjoyment of their self-centred desires will be the torment of the memory of what, in their experience of God's enlightening influence in their life on earth, they saw would be better than they were experiencing in *hell*.

The kind of situation which is abhorrent and *unnatural* to a person in whom God has given His nature, is pleasing and *natural* for the person who does not share His nature. The same experience is observed from different points of view and is expressed in different words.

The startling conclusion I have reached is that the statement by Paul that God *"gave them up* to the lusts of their own hearts ..." [1] that is, to satisfy the desires of their natural natures, **means the same as**, to be '*thrown into the lake* that burns with fire and brimstone', to suffer 'unquenchable thirst', where 'the worm never dies and where there will be weeping and gnashing of teeth'.

[1] Romans 1:24

12 Conclusion

For those who have been enlightened by God and those whose natures have been transformed by Him, the fulfilment of people's natural natures will be as spiritually abhorrent as would be physically to be thrown into eternal torment in a lake of fire and brimstone, experience unquenchable thirst and 'the worm that will not die'.

For those who die with their natural untransformed natures, *hell* will give them the freedom to be and do whatever they desire without the limitations of God influence or presence.

Stated in equation form:

To be 'given up' to the desires of one's natural nature = 'to be cast into the lake of fire and torment of hell'.

For 'unforgiven sinners' with natures that have not been changed in their lifetime, the punishment for the evil acts committed will be severe but just, and will end on completion. The fulfilling of the 'lusts of their own hearts' will be experienced for ever. An addition will probably be the memory of their experience of God's influence in their lifetime which they rejected. Cf the 'rich man' and Lazarus.

As Jesus stated it:

"For to everyone who has will more be given, and he will have an abundance. But from the one who has not, even what he has will be taken away." [1]

For the 'forgiven sinners', with natures that have been made God-like and with their sins — their short-comings from His perfect holiness — forgiven and forgotten, the prospect of eternity without God and without the fellowship of similarly transformed people, would indeed be like being thrown into a 'lake of fire and brimstone, suffering unquenchable thirst, and experiencing the 'worm which never dies' and 'weeping and gnashing of teeth'.

[1] Matthew 13:12

12 Conclusion

These are vivid physical pictures of real spiritual experiences as seen from God's point of view.

Paul expresses the sense of the words: *"the lusts of their hearts"* elsewhere as *"the pattern of this world"*.

"Do not be conformed to this world, but be transformed by the renewal of your mind, that by testing you may discern what is the will of God, what is good and acceptable and perfect."[1]

The term 'this world' is more fully translated as 'the pattern of this age'. To be conformed to 'this world' is to behave according to 'the pattern of this age', that is, to behave according to one's natural nature. The *"renewal of your mind"* is to conform to 'the pattern of God', that is, to behave according to one's 'born again' or 'divine nature'.

The Apostle John expands *"the pattern of this world"* to *"all that is in the world — the desires of the flesh and the desires of the eyes and pride in possessions."* [2]

Although the term 'the pattern of God' is not used in the Bible it expresses very well what is meant by "the new life of the Spirit" which Paul spelled out in Romans 6 and 7.

Using these terms, the following three equations illustrate the conclusion reached but expressed in other words. Watch for the plus (+) and minus (-) signs.

In this present world or age, 'the pattern of this age' and 'the pattern of God' operate together. Those with unchanged natures follow 'the pattern of this age' and those with 'born again' natures follow 'the pattern of God'. The Bible, people's consciences, observing the created universe, the Law of Moses and God's revelation in Jesus Christ, give clear indications of which kind of human behaviour in the world is according to which pattern. In the present environment both patterns operate at the same time but in different people.

This world = 'the pattern of this age' + 'the pattern of God'

[1] Romans 12:2 [2] 1 John 2 15

12 Conclusion

After the Great Judgement Seat of God, those whose natures have been changed by God imparting His 'divine nature' in them will be welcomed into *heaven*. The environment there will be entirely according to 'the pattern of God' in its fullness *minus*, that is, with no trace of 'the pattern of this age'. This can be represented as: Note '-' means 'minus'.

Heaven = 'the pattern of God' - 'the pattern of this age'

After the Great Judgement Seat, those whose natures have not been changed during their lifetime will be 'cast into' *hell*, that is, they will live according to 'the pattern of this age' minus any trace of 'the pattern of God'.

Hell = ' the pattern of this age' - 'the pattern of God'

In this present world everyone begins life by behaving according to 'the pattern of this age'. Then God introduces them to His pattern of living. When people respond to the Gospel and are 'born again' into the kingdom of God they begin to live according to 'the pattern of God'. After death and the Judgement Seat of God, people will go either (a) to *heaven* to behave according to 'the pattern of God' with no trace of 'the pattern of this age' or (b) to *hell* to behave according to 'the pattern of this age' with no trace of 'the pattern of God'.

It follows from this interpretation that we need look no further than this world now for indications of what *heaven* and *hell* will be like. Remove 'the pattern of this age' from life now and you have strong indications of what *heaven* will be like. Remove 'the pattern of God' from this world and you have very clear indications of what *hell* will be like.

Heaven and *hell* will be viewed differently by those whose natures have or have not been transformed by God during their lifetime.

12 Conclusion

An experience I had as a missionary in Rwanda illustrates this point. On one occasion I stood beside my car at the side of the road drinking a mug of coffee entranced by the magnificent view before me. Luscious green fields, grass and trees merged into Mount Muhabura on the other side of the valley. A local man was passing by. I pointed to the amazing beauty of the landscape before us. He replied: "It is not beautiful, the crop of millet was poor this year."

We were looking at the same scene but seeing different things. Our points of view were different. As a result, we experienced different emotions — mine was *enjoyment* of spectacular beauty; his was *grief*, for a failed crop.

Other events in Africa gave me vivid pictures of life approaching that of *heaven* and *hell*. As a missionary in Rwanda, in the latter stages of the East African Revival, I was in contact with people — African and missionary — who had experienced a deep conviction of the sin in their lives and what was, for them, the horror of life out of fellowship with God and with the prospect of eternity in *hell*. Then, in repenting of their sin and trusting in the sacrifice of Jesus, they experienced the utter joy of sins forgiven and the unclouded indwelling presence of God and fellowship with those who had been similarly revived. I came to understand in my own experience that unrepented sin becomes intolerable. The joy of love for God and for each other and the openness in relationships became very precious. It was a taste of heaven on earth, available for all those who know God's forgiveness and daily presence.

Some 40 years later a 'fellowship' of a different kind emerged in Rwanda. In the genocide of 1994, thousands of *hutu* killed *tutsi* and equally *tutsi* killed *hutu*. In bands of armed men, they enjoyed the united experience of killing.

12 Conclusion

Paul Rusesabagina was the manager of the hotel 'Mille Collines', the theme of the film 'Hotel Rwanda'. He wrote: "Something magical happens to you when you join a group, a feeling I can only describe as *freedom*. ... It is possible to lose oneself in the purpose of the collective effort; we embrace this feeling of being dissolved into something bigger because at our cores we are lonely. ... We thirst for that unity, the lost wholeness that we imagine we had before we were born. That feeling of warm acceptance we get inside a group is addictive; it is one of the most powerful human urges. And when your individuality is dissolved into the will of the pack you then become free to act in any way the pack directs. The thought of acting otherwise becomes as abhorrent as death. ... If nobody can find it within themselves to stand outside the group and find the inner strength to say no, then the mass of men will easily commit atrocities for the sake of keeping up appearances " [1]

I have myself witnessed a member of one of the ethnic groups brutally attacking a member of the other group. It happened both ways.

In both my experience of fellowship of Revival in Rwanda and that of the murdering gangs of the genocide period, the word *freedom* occurs. That seems to be the key to understanding the environments of *heaven* and *hell*. In both, people will have the *freedom to enjoy* to the full that which their different natures desire. Christians, whose natures are God-centred and 'righteous' can understand the difference between these freedoms. Non-Christians whose natures are self-centred and 'unrighteous' will not understand unless God enlightens their minds.

In truth, one man's *heaven* is another man's *hell!*
And vice versa!

[1] *An ordinary man* Paul Rusesabagina Bloomsbury pp 248-249

12 Conclusion

God is often portrayed as being gracious towards those who respond to His love but harsh to those who reject it. According to this view, He is happy to see the former enjoying the glorious environment of *heaven* while the latter suffer the eternal torment of *hell* which they deserve by their evil deeds and their rebellion against Him.

The true situation is more like that of loving parents who bring up their children to enjoy a happy home in which they give them the freedom to make up their own minds about their behaviour. They create an environment where obedience to their parents and loving relationships provide all that contributes to a happy childhood.

Many parents will have given their children a gift of money for them to use as they wish, only to see them spend it on rubbish. The parents will grieve to see their children enjoying things which, in their view, are valueless.

Then comes the time when the children leave their parents and form their own homes. Some keep in contact with their parents and model their family lives on their childhood experience. Others reject their parents, break off from them and create their own independent life styles.

It is not difficult to understand both the *joy* of the parents relationship with those of their children who share their life style, and their *grief* at observing those who, reject them and enjoy a life-style which, for them, would be unbearable.

How great must be the delight of God at the exercise of freedom by those who respond to His love, *and* how great His grief at the exercise of freedom by those who rebel against Him

"Have I any pleasure in the death of the wicked, declares the Lord GOD, and not rather that he should turn from his way and live?" [1]

[1] Ezekiel 18:23

12 Conclusion

When God created the first man and woman, Adam and Eve, the destiny He intended for them and for every one of their descendents was *heaven*. However, to enjoy and qualify for that eternal environment with God, they had to *choose* that rather than the alternative *hell*. The Good News of Jesus is the story of God creating people with Himself as the model, giving them freedom of choice and then doing everything possible to make every one's choice *heaven* rather than *hell,* short of forcing them to act against their natures. This included informing people of the joys of *heaven* and warning them of the *horrors* of hell.

This raises for me an important question. Does the understanding of *heaven* and *hell* and the interpretation of the biblical statements relative to them which I have outlined diminish the horror of *hell* to the extent that people would no longer fear it as their eternal destiny? If that is the case, then my interpretation is false. For:

"It is a fearful thing to fall into the hands of the living God." [1]

These are solemn words which must not be ignored. It would falsify the Gospel to reduce the fear of hell which the Bible clearly teaches. However, the more I have reflected on the implications of the views of *heaven* and *hell* presented here, the greater has been my conviction of the fearful, frightening destiny that is *hell*.

Rather than reduce the fear of *hell*, the opposite is true. The thought of an environment in which there is no God of love, no loving faithful relationships, no unselfish acts and all is directed by self-interest and futility, is appalling. The prospect of such an environment will surely be totally abhorrent to any one who has experienced and enjoyed honest dealings, loving relationships, mercy and justice.

[1] Hebrews 10:31

12 Conclusion

The question then arises. Is this understanding of the awfulness of *hell* one that makes sense only to the mind enlightened by the Spirit of God but is foolish to the 'unsaved'? Should, therefore, the biblical teaching of hell remain in the usual vivid, literal fearful physical terms for the benefit of the unbeliever?

I think not. The harm that arises from accepting the biblical descriptions of hell — lake of fire, brimstone, unquenchable thirst, the worm that will not die, eternal torment, in their literal senses — without understanding their spiritual significance is to fall into the trap of considering them as imaginary, grotesque ideas intended 'to put the fear of hell' into people. It is then only necessary to degrade the use of the term 'fear of hell' to describe a range of totally unrelated situations to reduce it to a meaningless fantasy promoted by bigoted, intolerant, narrow-minded extremists.

I believe that Christians need to wake up to this deception.

A major factor in my understanding of the destinies of *heaven* and *hell* has been the realisation of the *enjoyment* which many, if not most people gain in the evil they commit, by their *happiness* in pursuing spiritually futile activities, and by their *contentment* in leaving their Creator out of their thinking and behaviour ... all in the fulfillment of the desires of their 'natural' natures,

I do not claim that the conclusions I have reached have solved all the problems. The major one of the uncomfortable combination of ideas — the *love of God* in *heaven* and the eternal *torment* of those in *hell* — has been resolved.

I am convinced, however, that to proclaim the glories of *heaven* without spelling out the horrors of *hell,* from both points of view, is to diminish the Gospel.

Epilogue

To know brings the responsibility of acting in the light of knowledge. God gave Ezekiel a commission which was to apply not only to the prophet of Israel but to every Christian of the church grafted into Israel:
"So you, son of man, I have made a watchman for the house of Israel. Whenever you hear a word from my mouth, you shall give them warning from me." [1]

In parables, Jesus passed on the same message to the disciples:
"Everyone to whom much was given, of him much will be required." [2]

Jesus said more about *hell* than any other writer of the Bible. In parables about the kingdom of *heaven* there were warnings of *hell*. Why is it, therefore, that many preachers and teachers appear to ignore His warnings. His teaching on *heaven* and *hell* is part of the 'much' Christians are given, hence much will be required of them.

The experience of many Christians is that, although they have heard 'the word from God's mouth' through the written word, the Bible, they find it difficult to communicate that warning to others, even to those they know well.

[1] Ezekiel 3:17 [2] Luke 12:48

A problem, which was recognized at the beginning of this study, is that the warnings given in the Bible are couched in terms which sound to many people, even to Christians, to be scaringly, frighteningly and alarmingly vivid. To speak of 'the lake of fire and brimstone', the 'worm that will not die', the 'thirst that will not be quenched', the 'everlasting torment', is to frighten people rather than encourage them to respond to God's gracious loving invitation to respond to His offer of mercy and 'new birth' into His kingdom.

The important fact which emerges from this study of *heaven* and *hell,* is that the 'horror of hell' appears to be terrifying to those who have a 'love of the light' — a knowledge of the character and purposes of God, but is completely irrelevant and undaunting to those who do not have that 'light' and are, by definition, 'lovers of darkness'.

Reflecting on this issue suggests a number of ways in which the final destinies — *heaven* and *hell* — can be presented in realistic terms without in any way diminishing the horrifying alternative to *heaven* which *hell* represents.

Three principles are important in presenting the facts:

From the Apostle Paul:

(a) *"The natural person does not accept the things of the Spirit of God, for they are folly to him, and he is not able to understand them because they are spiritually discerned."* [1]

(b) *"My message was not in plausible words of wisdom, but in demonstration of the Spirit and of power, that your faith might not rest in the wisdom of men but in the power of God."* [2]

(c) *"And even if our gospel is veiled, it is veiled only to those who are perishing. In their case the god of this world has blinded the minds of the unbelievers, to keep them from seeing the light of the gospel of the glory of Christ, who is the image of God."* [3]

[1] 1 Corinthians 2:14 [2] 1 Corinthians 2:4-5 [3] 2 Corinthians 4:3

The following outline suggestions present biblical truths of *heaven* and *hell* in contexts which show them to be integral parts of the Gospel. Such presentations must include the prayer and the faith that God will enlighten the understanding of the hearers.

(1) The two natures

There is a clear biblical distinction between the natures of those who are 'born again' into the 'kingdom of God' and the natures of those who are not.

Being 'saved' from the 'family of Satan' to be a member of the 'family of God' is a transforming experience. It is far from some people's concept of simply a change of ideas or beliefs. It is this life-changing transformation which makes the Christian faith different from every other religion. The importance of this distinction between the 'saved' and the 'unsaved' lies in that:

(a) it defines a persons's relationship to God — He lives *in* 'born again' Christians and not only *with* them. He influences them from the 'inside' and not, as with non-Christians, from the 'outside' of them;

(b) it affects a person's behaviour in this life — A person who is 'saved from sin' lives no longer under the fear of law (I must not ...), to live under the impulse of 'grace' (I don't want to ...);

(c) it moulds his or her attitude to the authority of the Bible in all aspects of life — from creation, life now, to the end of history: the Judgement Seat of God.

(d) it determines the 'world view' of a person — the God-given understanding of the purpose of His creation and His working throughout history;

(e) it directs the nature and direction of the 'treasure' that everyone lays up for themselves, however unwittingly, in their daily lives.

(f) it establishes, during their life time, their final destinies of *heaven* or *hell*.

Viewed in the light of the total picture, the biblical statements about *heaven* and *hell* will be seen to be an integral part of the total Gospel and not an optional addition.

(2) 'Sowing' and 'reaping'

The 'glories of heaven' and the 'horrors of hell' are the reaping of what is sown during a person's lifetime

- for the Christian, sowing is a working out of a transformation from a 'natural *without* God' nature into a supernatural '*with* God within' nature being moulded during life into the model or image of Jesus. According to Paul it is to *"work out your own salvation with fear and trembling."* [1]

- for the non-Christian, sowing is the 'perishing' or hardening of the 'natural without God' nature into an even more self-centred, un-godlike nature. This is the fruit of choosing not to believe God-given truth, by repeatedly ignoring the conscience, by suppressing conviction of sin and by acting in ways which are known to be wrong.

The first part of the well-known words of Jesus are often quoted. The second part is essential for the whole picture:

"For God so loved the world that he gave his only Son, that whoever believes in him should not perish but have eternal life. For God did not send his Son into the world to condemn the world, but in order that the world might be saved through him. Whoever believes in him is not condemned, but whoever does not believe is condemned already, because he has not believed in the name of the only Son of God." [1]

The end point of 'perish' is *hell* and that of 'eternal life' is *heaven*. As Jesus said:

"Whoever believes in him is not condemned, but whoever does not believe is condemned already."

---
[1] Philippians 2:12

The path to *heaven* or *hell* begins at birth. When a child begins to understand the difference between right and wrong he or she is on the path to *hell* and will continue on it unless there is a turning off the road. This life is a preparation for the eternal hereafter. What people are and do now has consequences for life after death. The most common presentation of *heaven* and *hell* concentrates on them as final 'reaping' destinations. Equally important is the preparation for them in the 'sowing' in this life.

* *'Sowing' for those 'born again' into the 'kingdom of God'* includes:

(a) embracing a new 'world view' in which the universe, the world and other people are viewed from God's point of view. The process of history is the working out of His purposes for the people He brought into being.

(b) being a testimony to the reality of God as a living presence, forgiving sin, enabling victory over sin, and empowering for service for Him and being a witness to the non-Christian world.

(c) forming a community in which the loving, caring relationships which God's nature produces are lived out for all to see and note that 'they have been with Jesus', and in so doing, give a taste of the environment of *heaven*.

(d) in weakness and suffering, in personal tragedy, in national disaster and distress, and especially in persecution, to witness to the power of God to give peace and hope.

(e) the 'laying up of treasure' by all work and activities being done for God and in His name, whatever may be the human reason — work for a living, care for the sick, relief for the needy and acts of compassion.

(f) the sure hope of God's 'well done good and faithful service' in the coming day when everyone will stand before Him to be judged for what they have done in the lives.

[1] John 3:16-18

* '*Sowing*' *for those not 'born again into the 'kingdom of God':*
   (a) The steady 'perishing' of the character due to repeated rejections of God and His word, a 'hardening of the heart' to the Gospel, an increasing 'blindness to evident truth', e.g a God-created universe, and a deadening of the conscience.
   (b) The committing of acts which anger God because they counter His loving purposes for every one — causing suffering to others by the pursuit of one's self-interest, greed, oppression and lust for power and applause.
   (c) A way of life which increasingly leaves God out of account and pursues spiritually futile activities which gratify self-centred desires and pander to pride.
   Presented in this way, *heaven* and *hell* are the *reaping* of what is *sown* during people's lifetimes. An important element in this preparation for the 'life to come' is the evidence available for all with eyes to see, of the effects in individual and social life now of both the 'nature without God' in the evil and futility in the world, and of the 'nature with God' in genuinely Christian communities. Sowing for *heaven* and *hell* is taking place now in situations which give ample evidence of the final environments.

(3) The broad and the narrow ways
   Both in the Bible and in secular society, life is often portrayed as a journey along a road. As time passes and events happen to a person, so life is pictured as 'walking' along the metaphorical 'road of life'. In the physical world, to go along one road rather than another at a fork or cross-roads requires choice, a change of surface on which one is walking and a change of destination. To walk along a road with no thought given to where it leads is clearly senseless.
   Forks or cross-roads imply that decisions have to be made about which of the possible roads to follow, and the

consequences recognized of going along the chosen road. Jesus used the metaphor of life as walking along a road with particular reference to the most important junction in the road for every person. This junction can be presented in two ways:

(a) Walking along a road which ends in a fork — one way leading to *heaven* and the other to *hell*.

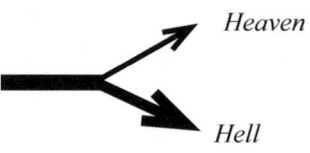

(b) walking along a broad road leading to *hell* and coming to a turning off the road during life leading to *heaven*.

The biblical picture is the second, not the first. The choice is not to go *either* to heaven or to hell at physical death. *Hell* is the end of the road a person is on now unless there is a turning off during a person's life from that road to the one that leads to *heaven*. Jesus spelled it out:

"You can enter God's Kingdom only through the narrow gate. The highway to hell is broad, and its gate is wide for the many who choose that way." [1]

The Apostle Peter referred to the turning off the main road as being 'called out of darkness into light':

Christians are:

*"... a chosen race, a royal priesthood, a holy nation, a people for his own possession, that you may proclaim the excellencies of him who **called you out** of darkness into his marvellous light. Once you were not a people, but now you are God's people; once you had not received mercy, but now you have received mercy."* [2]

The Apostle Paul refers to the road junction as a transfer of nationality from one kingdom to another:

[1] Matthew 7:13 (New Living)   [2] 1 Peter 2:9-10

*"He (God the Father) has **delivered us** from the domain of darkness and transferred us to the kingdom of his beloved Son, in whom we have redemption, the forgiveness of sins."* [1]

From these quotations it is clear that 'turning off from the highway to *hell*' and joining the 'narrow way to *heaven*' is more than having a change of mind about religious ideas. It is becoming a spiritually different person. It is:

(a) leaving the citizenship of Satan and therefore, of sin, and becoming a citizen of the kingdom of God:

(b) belonging to a different race — God's chosen race — sharing His 'divine nature';

(c) leaving a 'domain of darkness' for a 'domain of light', in which Jesus is the light;

(d) walking along a different road, a road which leads to *heaven*, not continuing on the road that leads to *hell*.

Biblical teaching on *heaven* and *hell* gives a very strong warning to people not to leave their choice of 'turning off from the 'highway to *hell*' too late.

Now is the right time.

In the beginning, God ...   In the end, God ...

The Christian faith is the only religion in the world in which its Creator reveals the truth of history of the past and lets His people know what history will be in the future before it happens.

As God has revealed His-story to us, there are three principle series of events which divide time as we know it: (a) The *beginning* — creation of the universe and people; (b) the *centre* — the life, death, resurrection and ascension of Jesus, God as Man, and (c) the *end* — the final completion of all that He set out to do and which He has revealed to the objects of His action — us, you and me.

[1] Colossians 1:13-14

(a) Creation and the Fall of the foundation members of the human race — Adam and Eve.

On planet earth, God set in motion the greatest project ever — to bring into being spirit beings who would be like Him in many ways, but not equal to Him, and give them the possibility of *choosing* to be adopted into His family to live for ever in the perfect environment of *heaven.*

Through two events which were His *permissive* but not His *active will*, the first man and woman and all their descendents were banished to an alternative family to His, that of Satan.[1] They became spiritually dead — separated from the life of God and were therefore outside His kingdom.

God then influenced the descendants of Adam and Eve to want to be in His kingdom rather than that of Satan by revealing Himself and His purposes to them through prophets and writings. There was, however, a major obstacle to anyone being adopted into the family of God — everyone sins, that is, acts in ways which fall short of His perfect holiness. Dealing with that obstacle was the purpose of the second major series of events in history.

(b) The life, death, resurrection and ascension of Jesus Christ.

In these events Jesus did what human beings on their own could not do. When a person sins against God, he or she cannot turn the clock back and *not* do what they did. That act makes it impossible for them to be adopted into God's family. Jesus did what is humanly impossible. Briefly, Jesus did something for every person who believes in Him which has the same effect as would happen if the clock could be turned back and the person had not sinned. In God's sight, that person becomes as if he or she had not sinned and God could live His life in them.

[1] See Appendix B

However, the experience of having seen what sin is and its effects, repented of it, turned away from it and trusted in what Jesus did, is the point of the whole action.

The immediate consequences of this act is that it divides the world into two groups — those who *choose* to reject being in the family of Satan and be adopted into the family of God and those who do not.

For about two thousand years, the record of history until then — the Bible — the Gospel and the *choice* God offers people, have been made known in every country of the world. That leads to the final great series of events which concerns the final fulfilment of God's great project and, in particular, what happens to those two groups of people.

(c) The coming again of Jesus, the universal acknowledgement of God as the only God, the final judgement and the establishment of heaven and hell.

As most of what *heaven* and *hell* mean has been dealt with, it remains to point out the great importance of including all the information about these final destinies in the presentation of the Gospel.

As '*in the beginning* ...' God set the scene by creating the universe and people in such a way that He could offer them a *unique choice* — a change of final destination — from *hell* to *heaven*. '*In the centre*' God made the *unique choice* possible. "*In the end...*" God will direct people to the destination of their choice.

What are men or women really like?

The most common view of what people are really like appears to be that everyone has two sides to their natures, Many people are decent, good living and generous individuals as they demonstrate the good side of their natures. Other people act in ways which are unsociable and hurt their fellows as they give way to the bad side of their natures.

According to this understanding of human nature, people need to be disciplined to behave according to the good side of their nature rather than the bad side.

This is not the teaching of the Bible. According to biblical teaching, people behave according to their 'natural'. 'fallen natures', unless restrained by God working through their consciences or through the social order when God based. Jesus made the connection between attitude — the desires of a person's nature — and behaviour.

"But I say to you that everyone who is angry with his brother will be liable to judgment; whoever insults his brother will be liable to the council; and whoever says, 'You fool!' will be liable to the hell of fire." [1]

To say to someone: "You fool", may not sound very bad but it is, in fact, the expression of an attitude of superiority of one person over another. That attitude is an expression of a person's natural nature and that puts them in danger of hell. It is an uncomfortable teaching of Jesus that all that is 'ungodly' in a person comes from their natures and not from their circumstances. Jesus said:

"Hear me, all of you, and understand: There is nothing outside a person that by going into him can defile him, but the things that come out of a person are what defile him. ... Do you not see that whatever goes into a person from outside cannot defile him, since it enters not his heart but his stomach, and is expelled?... For from within, out of the heart of man, come evil thoughts, sexual immorality, theft, murder, adultery, coveting, wickedness, deceit, sensuality, envy, slander, pride, foolishness. All these evil things come from within, and they defile a person." [2]

The Apostle Paul stated the same fact using the term *'the flesh'*, that is, natural human nature, to express what Jesus meant by *"from within, out of the heart of man"*.

[1] Matthew 5:22 [2] Mark 7:14-23

"Now the works of the flesh are evident: sexual immorality, impurity, sensuality, idolatry, sorcery, enmity, strife, jealousy, fits of anger, rivalries, dissensions, divisions, envy, drunkenness, orgies, and things like these. I warn you, as I warned you before, that those who do such things will not inherit the kingdom of God." [1]

Every one of the sinful acts listed here and elsewhere in the New Testament comes into one or other of the categories which 'fall short of the glory of God': *unclean* — less than perfect holiness, *false or deceitful* — less than perfect 'light', truth and openness, and *shameful or detestable* — less than blameless, honourable, loving.

In contrast, Paul went on to list the characteristics of the nature of the person with God's imparted 'divine nature'.

"But the fruit of the Spirit is love, joy, peace, patience, kindness, goodness, faithfulness, gentleness, self-control; against such things there is no law. ... For the desires of the flesh are against the Spirit, and the desires of the Spirit are against the flesh, for these are opposed to each other, to keep you from doing the things you want to do ... And those who belong to Christ Jesus have crucified the flesh with its passions and desires. [2]

It is a person's nature which determines what he or she is like and it is that nature which will decide which of the two destinies awaits him or her. In this life Christians can choose which of their natures they obey.

It's not fair?

It is not difficult to imagine those whose lives appear to be 'saintly' in doing many good works and helping others enjoying the environment of *heaven*. It is equally not difficult to imagine those who have committed grievous crimes against their fellows suffering the just punishment they deserve and the eternal environment of *hell*. But what about

---

[1] Galatians 5:19-21   [2] Galatians 5:22-24

the many people who appear to have committed no serious crime, who have performed many generous acts and who have acted with much apparent honesty?

It is important to distinguish between the evil acts for which God will, in His anger, punish people and the rejection of life in the regime of His kingdom.

Imagine a family in which the parents insist on perfect cleanness before their children enter the house. However, if, after playing outside, before they enter the door, they confess to something about them which is dirty, the parents promise to clean them up to fit them to enter.

Two of their children go out to play. One, a boy, has a small dirty mark on his shirt caused by a ball which hit him. He tries to enter the house. The parents refuse him entry. The other child, a girl, returns to the house covered with mud and with not an item of clothing clean. She calls to their parents who come out and completely clean her up.

The girl appreciates such an act of mercy while the boy complains at such harsh and unfair treatment for such a trivial offence. The dirty mark was hardly noticeable. Surely that should not have deserved him being excluded from the house in the same way as his sister was!

The difference between the two is not one of degree of uncleanness, but of acceptance or otherwise of the regime of their parents. The criterion for entrance into the home is total acceptance of that regime not the degree of their falling short of it.

So it is with *heaven* and *hell*. Those who will be received into heaven will be those who accept the regime offered by God, however much they have fallen short of the 'perfect holiness' required. Those who will be 'given up' to be 'thrown into' hell will be those who, however good they may have been, reject God's regime.

Signs of the times

When a group of Jewish leaders came to Jesus *"to test him, they asked him to show them a sign from heaven."* They were obviously looking for some miraculous demonstration of supernatural power. Jesus replied:

"When it is evening, you say, 'It will be fair weather, for the sky is red.' And in the morning, 'It will be stormy today, for the sky is red and threatening.' You know how to interpret the appearance of the sky, but you cannot interpret the signs of the times." [1]

Jesus refused to perform a miraculous act to satisfy their curiosity. Instead He pointed to the evidence that was already there: 'the signs of the times'. It is most commonly assumed that the 'sign of the times' Jesus referred to related to the end of the age and to the second coming of Jesus. However, there are also 'the signs of the times' which relate to the future judgement of God on everyone who has ever lived on earth and to their destinies of *heaven* and *hell*.

Jesus said,

"Blessed are the poor in spirit for theirs is the kingdom of heaven. ... Blessed are those who are persecuted for righteousness sake for theirs is the kingdom of heaven. ... Blessed are you when others revile you and persecute you and utter all kinds of evil against you falsely on my account. Rejoice and be glad, for your reward is great in heaven," [2]

History records many persecuted, reviled and falsely accused people who will be joyfully welcomed into *heaven*. It is right that Christians should rejoice in their future vindication. At the same time, history records many persecutors, revilers and false accusers whose final destiny of *hell* is equally clear. One of the 'signs of the times', particularly in these days of mass media, is the record of the many who appear to enjoy robbing the poor, burning down churches,

[1] Matthew 16:1-3 [2] Matthew 5:10-12

brutally ill-treating and killing Christians. In almost every sphere of life there are signs which support the biblical truth that evil will increase as the day of judgement approaches.

The 20th century witnessed the *Gulags* (labour camps) of Russia, the Jewish holocaust, the 'killing fields' of Cambodia, in which, at the command of ruthless dictators and with the cooperation of willing assistants, millions were made to endure intense suffering and many were killed. Less dramatic but no less devastating has been the ruthless shattering of lives by business deals, financial arrangements, heartless subjection of people to commercial interests, and the making slaves of the helpless of one area for the exploitation of another. Even in school playgrounds children suffer the bullying effects of the same natures.

The application of the parables of Jesus to the present day situation is a good example of observing the 'signs of the times'. In the parable of the sower of good seed in which weeds appeared, Jesus quoted the servants of the owner of the field saying: *"Master, did you not sow good seed in your field? How then does it have weeds?"* [1]

The servants were rightly reading the 'signs of the times'. They discerned not only that there were 'weeds' growing among the 'good seed', but that the two were so intermixed that it would be impossible to distinguish one from the other sufficiently to separate them. However, Jesus gave them the meaning of the 'signs of the times' that they had observed.

"Let both grow together until the harvest ... The harvest is the close of the age, and the reapers are angels. Just as the weeds are gathered and burned with fire, so will it be at the close of the age. The Son of Man will send his angels, and they will gather out of his kingdom all causes of sin and all law-breakers, and throw them into the fiery furnace.

In that place there will be weeping and gnashing of teeth. Then the righteous will shine like the sun in the kingdom of their Father. He who has ears, let him hear." [1]

The picture of 'good seed' all mixed up with 'weeds' can be observed today in every branch of government, commerce, industry, social life, sport and entertainment. This is surely a 'sign of the times' which shouts for a proclamation of the 'harvest' which God will one day order to execute justice on the whole world. Then the 'good seed' will be welcomed into God's 'barn' — *heaven*, and the weeds bound so there is no escape to be cast into *hell*.

Not to recognize these signs is to declare an incomplete Gospel. The signs of *heaven* and *hell* are with us now.

A parable from the life of Jesus.

Using the language of the Bible and its meaning in today's language to present biblical truth is important, but it is not sufficient without reliance on God to enlighten darkened minds. In presenting the truths of God's word, we face two obstacles: minds which do not naturally understand and accept spiritual truths, and, spirit powers which actively blind people's minds to the truth. In the light of these facts, an important factor in presenting the truths of *heaven* and *hell* is the relationship of the presenter to God, his or her recognition of the spiritual adversaries and the impossibility of combatting them solely by human reasoning or rhetoric.

"For we do not wrestle against flesh and blood, but against principalities, against powers, against the rulers of the darkness of this age, against spiritual hosts of wickedness in the heavenly places." [2]

The first miracle which Jesus performed was turning water into wine at a wedding feast. [3] The advice of Mary, the mother of Jesus to the servants was significant: *"Do whatever he tells you."* At the word of Jesus, *"fill the jars with*

[1] Matthew 13:27 [2] Ephesians 6:12 [3] John 2:1-9

water" the servants did just that. Then Jesus said: *"Now draw some out and take it to the master of the feast."* Again, they did just that. *"When the master of the feast tasted the water it had become wine."* What had been 'water' to the servants became 'wine' to the master of the feast who tasted it and to the guests who shared his experience.

The servants 'filled the jars with water' and 'drew some out' but it was Jesus who turned the water into wine.

So it is with the biblical teaching on *heaven* and *hell*. We are to 'fill ourselves' with the information the Bible provides. We are to 'pour it out to the listeners'. It is, however, God who performs the miracle of 'turning the water into wine. Only God can turn 'water' — knowledge learned from the Bible and made our own, into the 'wine' of the understanding and experience of the listeners.

Given this understanding we became 'servants' entrusted with life-changing information and, as Paul stated it:

"Therefore, we are ambassadors for Christ, God making his appeal through us. We implore you on behalf of Christ, be reconciled to God." [1]

And Jesus: *"Therefore you also be ready, for the Son of Man is coming at an hour you do not expect."* [2]

To be ready and prepared for the final destinies of *heaven* and *hell* is the most important occupation of every living man and woman.

Note that those who will enjoy the environment of *hell* will originally have been no different from those who will enjoy the environment of *heaven*. Something happens to the natures of people while on earth which changes them from enjoying the freedom of 'wallowing in the mud in the valley', like the pig, to enjoying the 'freedom of the skies' like the eagle. Jesus referred to this as being 'born again', theologians refer to it as 'regeneration'.

[1] 2 Corinthians 5:20   [2] Matthew 24:44

Anyone who has experienced on earth a glimpse of 'life in heaven' and *desires it,* would find that the environment of *hell* like being 'cast into a lake of fire', experiencing the torment of 'unquenchable thirst' and enduring an undying memory like a 'worm that will not die'. The horror of *hell* is meaningless to everyone who, by their natures, do not *desire* the environment of *heaven.*

Most hymns and Christian songs which refer to the end of this world as we know it now, refer to *heaven* in glowing terms of triumph. Very few mention the alternative *hell.* An exception is a hymn by Andrew Reed (1787-1862), an English minister of the Congregational Church in the early 19th century. It makes a fitting end to this Epilogue:

> There is an hour when I must part
>   With all I hold most dear;
> And life with its best hopes will then
>   As nothingness appear.
>
> There is an hour when I must sink
>   Beneath the stroke of death,
> And yield to Him, who gave it first,
>   My struggling, vital breath.
>
> There is an hour when I must stand
>   Before the judgment seat,
> And all my sins, and all my foes,
>   In awful vision meet.
>
> There is an hour when I must look
>   On one eternity;
> And nameless woe, or blissful life,
>   My endless portion be.
>
> O Saviour then, in all my need,
>   Be near, be near to me;
> And let my soul by steadfast faith
>   Find life and heaven in Thee.

Appendix A

The two natures in the three environments:

This present age

The natures of people	The Environment
 'Born' naturally separated from God 'Born again' united to God **'Light' & 'darkness' co-exist**	People experience the invisible presence and influence of both God and Satan. God's revelation, the Bible is available to them, to inform them of who He is, what His purposes are in creating the universe and people and what He has done to give them the choice of whether or not to be 'born again' into His kingdom

Heaven

A person's 'born again' nature	The Environment
 A person who dies having been 'born again' and united with God **'Light' alone exists**	People experience the intimate presence of God without the limitations of their 'old nature'. Their activities are indescribably more wonderful than human minds can understand at present.

Hell

A person's 'old nature'	The Environment
 A person who dies separated from God and remains so for ever **'Darkness' alone exists**	People no longer experience the presence and influence of God but indulge in their self-centred desires with only the memory of what might have been to limit their enjoyment.

Appendix B

Why people are born outside of 'kingdom of God'?

The first recorded preaching of Jesus was: *"Repent, for the kingdom of heaven is near."* [1] Why were his hearers — and hence us — not in that kingdom to begin with?

Before the beginning of time, there was only God — a family of like, but individual God-Persons. They were not structurally one Being, but three separate Persons who were bound together by *light* — everything in the open, and by *love* — total commitment to each other. They decided together to add to their family other intelligent beings who would not be 'God' as they were, but would be capable of sharing their *light* and their *love*. However, the three God-Persons were bound together because they, each individually, *wanted* to be. That meant they *chose* to be a God-Family. The 'beings' to be added to their family would, therefore, have to be there because that was *their choice*.

The first step in God's programme was to create spirit beings called angels and give them a certain freedom in their thinking. We learn of what happened from two passages in the Old Testament which were addressed to the chief rebel angel Satan or Lucifer. The principle was used by Jesus when He said to His disciple Peter, *"Get behind me Satan."* Although He was talking to Peter He was really addressing Satan. So it was with the King of Tyre [1] and Babylon. [2]

A third of the angels followed Lucifer or Satan, to rebel against God's 'light' and 'love'. They were banished to create a new, alternative family to that of God, that of Satan. The important point about this 'alternative family' was that, *no one could be in both* families — God's and Satan's.

[1] Ezekiel 28:2,11-15 [2] Isaiah 14:12-15

God then, on planet earth, created a new kind of being — men and women — *us*. We are different from angels in that they are only *spirit* bodies, and we are different from animals in that they are only *physical* bodies. We are both *physical* and *spirit* beings.

The first man and woman, Adam and Eve, were given a large measure of freedom but with one restriction.[1] They, like Satan and his fallen angels, rebelled against God's restriction and they were banished to the 'family of Satan'.

From then onwards everyone, was and now is, born into the 'family of Satan', that is, *out of* the family of God. No one could *choose* to be in God's family if already in it.

Now, God and Satan are present but they are hidden for a special reason. The God-Family of Father, Son and Holy Spirit have done everything possible to present life in their family as the best that could ever be for everyone. And they have given Satan as much scope as he needs to present what life for ever in his family would mean. God and Satan are hidden in order that a person's choice of continuing in the family of Satan or accepting God's offer of being adopted into His family shall be *entirely free*.

For those who *choose* to be in God's family, life with Him will be far more wonderful than it could be if they had been born into His perfect family to begin with and never sinned against Him. As in Jesus' parable, [2] they will share the joy of the home coming to the waiting loving father of the prodigal son who had seen evil and rejected it, rather than endure the self-righteous protests of the elder brother.

For a person to have experienced being in the 'family of Satan' and then *choose* to reject it and be adopted into the 'family of God' leads to a much more intimate love relationship with Him than would be possible otherwise.

[1] Genesis 2:16-17 [2] Luke 15:11-32

Appendix C

'Born again' into God's kingdom.

It may be that you, a reader, are aware that you are an 'unforgiven sinner' and that if your nature is not changed your destiny will be *hell*. If you have the desire to be changed that means that, unknown to you, perhaps, God is already drawing you to Himself and working to enable you to be 'born again' into His kingdom. Jesus said,

"No one can come to me unless the Father who sent me draws him. And I will raise him up on the last day." [1]
"All that the Father gives me will come to me, and whoever comes to me I will never cast out." [2]

That promise of Jesus is for you as well as for everyone else. To 'come to Him' is to recognize that He is present with you now and to tell to Him in whatever is your language and in whatever words, that you have repented of your sin — changed your mind about every way in which you have fallen short of His perfect standard — that you believe that in dying on the Cross Jesus took on Himself your sin, and you invite Him to come into your life.

You may find it helpful to read the following prayer and make it your own where that is true for you.

O God, I believe that you are the God of the Bible and that what is written there is true. I have sinned against you many times and I am sorry for what I have done. I am trusting now in what Jesus did for me when He died on the cross and I ask you to come into my life and to change me into what you planned for me to be. Help me to live for you for the rest of my life.

[1] John 6:44 [2] John 6:37